Messages from a Doctor in the Fourth Dimension

Vol. 2

(Volume 1 is available from the
publishers £4.95)

Dr. Karl Nowotny

Messages from a Doctor in the Fourth Dimension

Vol. 2

by

Dr. Karl Nowotny

Regency Press (London & New York) Ltd.
125 High Holborn, London WC1V 6QA

ISBN 0 7212 0867 3

Printed and bound in Great Britain by
Buckland Press Ltd., Dover, Kent.

Contents

The medium, Bertha, had barely entered my home when Dr Nowotny came though. I must add that the medium had no idea what I wanted and never knew him. Bertha is a speaking medium who works while fully conscious; she does not go into trance. Anxiously I waited for concrete evidence that I was not being hoaxed and deceived. My friend who brought the medium took this message in shorthand, so I am able to reproduce it word for word:

"I purposely come for only a short while. I do not come because I have been summoned, but because I have the desire to make a brief visit.

"It will be a long time until we meet here. This is why one should never think about the departure from the material world, but always only of life and the obligation to do one's duty so one can pass through the high portals into the dazzlingly radiant hall with a clear conscience.

"People live in the dark; they do not want to see clearly. But when we have passed through the door we are enlightened and are happy that life on earth is behind us. There is a world beyond. For me it is this world. Oh, how short human life is! It is over so quickly. One must be strong and not falter in one's plans, not succumb to earthly desires, but be happy, always seeing the good side of things. Sadness makes us weak and weary for every type of work.

"I can only say I am content and do not regret that I had to terminate my life. I had good friends. I am happy to have had them."

In answer to my question, "What are you doing now, doctor?" came the reply: "I have as much to do as when I was alive. Many people come and want my advice, but they don't follow it. I have given a lot of people encouragement and tried to strengthen them. They pay no attention after they have left me. They are like children leaving school. They don't think about the lesson and forget what they have learned."

If his first words encouraged me to think that everything was in order, the last sentence convinced me completely because these were the exact ones he often used to round off his lectures at the adult evening classes.

Subsequently I made several trips to Budapest and the medium Bertha in order to maintain contact and to receive more such pleasant messages. It was a great success, but the wish for constant contact grew steadily stronger. I plucked up courage and asked through the medium if Dr Nowotny would not try to write with my hand, as I knew about automatic writing.

In October 1966 we tried this for the first time. After two days I could receive messages, albeit slowly, without the medium. The writing grew steadily stronger and faster. In April 1967 I began this work.

The first volume comprised 116 pages of manuscript. Dr Nowotny said much more was to follow. The text is transcribed word for word from the manuscript.

I conclude with Dr Nowotny's wish, "May this work be an incentive for doctors and all interested readers to guide people along the right path, to show them the value of a good philosophy of life and give them peace and confidence."

The medium Grete.

Introduction

IN the first volume of my work, I mentioned that man is constantly in touch with infinity and has to take this fact into consideration in all life's situations.

It is such a vast field it must seem impossible to describe it from every angle so every reader has the feeling I have written this specifically for him with particular reference to his life, his tasks and his fate.

It is risky to imply that such a wish can be granted; that everybody will find something to interest only him, that seems to apply only to him.

For a person must learn that the community is all–important. Therefore, it is essential that everybody is familiar with as many areas of it as possible. Only in this way, through comparison and contemplation, will he be able to form a personal and objective opinion and see every situation in life in its proper perspective. At first glance this may seem very roundabout, but many a person will soon realise how valuable it is for everybody to study the problems of earthly existence over and over again, always from a different and fresh point of view.

What strikes people – and what was hitherto unknown to them – is how to examine earthly problems from the more elevated viewpoint of the world beyond. And it is precisely this which must become more generally known if the experiences of life are to be properly assessed and understood.

This is why, in volume 2, I continue where volume 1 ended. I will do the same with volume 3.

Have patience if you do not find the answers to questions that affect you immediately. I am convinced that nobody will put aside my writings without admitting they have caused him to reflect to what fundamentals I have outlined, and whether it bears critical examination.

What I explain and write about is based on my absolute knowledge. It needs no scientific proof even if your point of view is that this is precisely what is lacking. It will not be refuted by anybody who is schooled in the study of psychic science and has received evidence of life after death and the eternal, immortal existence of spirit and soul.

Therefore, accept the following chapters with the same goodwill you accorded volume 1. Know that I always mean well. Never tire of seeking the path and keeping to it with all the means at your disposal. It will lead you to a sound and normal philosophy of life.

Fate and its aspects in life.

WE last spoke about "understanding" and "forgiving" and said that children must be taught it early in life. Many mothers will ask how this is to be done. It is not difficult. Admittedly the child will not grasp the expressions "understanding" and "forgiving," although it will soon understand their meaning if, when the occasion arises, it is told that one understands what it wants, and why the wish either can or cannot be granted.

An understanding in a positive sense is naturally always better than one associated with a refusal. Instead of "forgiving," one will just not be angry and this must be emphasised. There are so many occasions in everyday life when this point of view can be applied.

An example is always the best teacher. A father who demands that his child always forgives without anger while he flies into a rage at the drop of a hat and threatens a hiding – or actually gives it – will never be a good influence. For a child tends to imitate what it sees rather than what it is told. Attention must also be paid as to in how far the child's personal tendencies indicate an automatic predisposition to correct behaviour. So much for the education of a child.

It is more difficult for the adult who had no good example in his childhood and had to pay dearly for every misdemeanor. With such people it depends whether the tendencies and experiences of previous incarnations are such that they find the right way due to a positive attitude, or whether the person, whose frame of mind is still underdeveloped, wants to revenge himself for the wrong done to him. How many bad deeds and crimes can be traced back to this! Practically all.

I advise that the background of such a criminal be examined . . . and invariably this statement will be borne out. As I have already said, here is a weak soul, unable to cope with negative influences – for it is only this. He cannot free himself either internally or externally from the unhealthy aggregate of conditions. His was by no means an arbitrary stellar constellation.

It is written in the infinite laws that all difficulties have first to be conquered and overcome before further progress can be made. But it does not mean that a person has to find the way alone. Those who are more developed than he are in duty bound to extend a helping hand. Of course, nobody can be forced to accept help. His free will enables him to ask for help and accept it when it is offered.

Fate cannot do exactly as it will with people, being only that which is good, pleasant or difficult, according to the established laws of Divine Omnipotence. It is given to man as a foundation in earthly existence. His free will allows him either to use and enjoy the benefits, according to his own discretion, or suffer and conquer the hardships in order to make spiritual progress.

"Man cannot escape his fate" is a well-known phrase. But it is only a phrase and incorrect. Life would not be interesting if we only had to live through a series of incarnations without having any influence on their course and development. To be sure, the salient characteristics cannot be wished away or circumvented. A person who attaches too much value to material possessions will perhaps just have to live in poverty-stricken conditions in another incarnation, in order to learn how much he really needs. Both poverty-stricken conditions and excessive riches of a previous life are determined by fate. They only indicate the foundation to build upon and exploit for the progress of the spirit.

Somebody may be excessively rich in earthly life, but it avails him little if he doesn't know how to use his wealth properly. On the contrary, he will retard his progress more than the person who bears a life of hardship, misery or sickness with dignity and equanimity, not to say thankfulness.

Many a person is unhappy about his wretched fate and only recognises its value after he has reached his goal and realises it was a wonderful basis for his incorporeal progress. When people understand that material possessions are only a blessing provided they do not exceed a modest limit or, should they be available in excessive measure, that they must be used for the community as a whole, then envy and greed will no longer dominate thought and cause as much restlessness and uncertainty as they do now.

A clean sweep still has to be made of colossal errors. Why,

according to earthly opinion must important men at the head of a state or a country possess an immense fortune, more than any of their subjects? There is no reason for this. It is sufficient that they are maintained at state cost and do not have to provide for their livelihood. To heap up material possessions, thereby often depriving the people of the basic elements of life, is stupid and useless. Of course, the opinion that riches, and only riches, bring happiness is still widespread.

But gradually people are beginning to understand that this is wrong, not least after catastrophes which demolish material possessions. Many a person has considered such a loss a release and realised that happiness in life is not centered around them.

As long as a wealthy man is held in higher esteem than a man of modest means, mankind is forced to be a slave to mammon and relegate ideal values to the background.

Once again it is primarily doctors who have to bear this in mind. Do not exaggerate the financial benefits you obtain from your calling and your career! Accept people as they are. Strip away material differences. Understand that everybody has the same right to your help whether he be rich or poor, but that particularly those who are without means need it more than the wealthy. This does not mean that a rich man needs less help. It is just that – as already established – material conditions are not a measure of the spiritual maturity and progress of a person. And earthly honours and influential positions by no means indicate a parallel degree of spiritual development.

Just for the record, a spiritual stage of development is not the same as intellectual development in the earthly sense, which is development in the realm of knowledge. It is – and remains – development of the spirit entity; knowledge and wisdom combined with all-embracing love.

Consider great scholars and artists or great politicians and statesmen and check in how far they fulfil these requirements. Only very few do. Most of them are content to dedicate themselves to their material achievements. Their souls are neglected and play no part – or very little – in their careers.

As soon as the principles for assessing a person are really accepted, these people will also be judged correctly. Because of this they will be obliged to control their lives and not place themselves above others only on account of their advanced and abundant knowledge.

A great deal of modesty and self-criticism is required here. Should arrogance prevent a person from applying these criteria, it is again a psychiatrist who must point him in the right direction.

Why do I enjoin a doctor to do this? Because a one-sided life is an indication of sickness. One day such improper conduct will cause the soul to renounce its duty.

Great artists, statesmen and scholars comprise a large section of a neurologist's patients. It is not an excess of work that brings them to him, but an incorrect attitude to life and a mistaken estimation of their own personalities.

Earlier on I drew attention to the development of the intellect and the consequent neglect of the soul. This results in an imbalance because the intellect develops quicker than the soul. If such an erring person is to be cured, he must learn to acknowledge this fact, and bring his intellectual activity closer to his emotional life.

This is not easy because intellectuals are very wilful and not receptive to outside influence.

We stop today and continue tomorrow with thoughts about education, not only of the child, but also of adults who were deprived of a healthy education in their youth. It is an extensive subject with many facets.

The value of spiritual progress.
Self-education and spiritual guides.

TODAY I want to discuss what people should do if they doubt that their opinion of things and individuals around them is correct.

This is very important because a wrong outlook on life can produce unfavourable consequences and impede progress. Not many people consider it necessary or even worthwhile to think about spiritual progress, because they are convinced they will only live once on earth. They consider it not only unnecessary but also inconvenient to worry about an uncertain and unknown life in the world beyond while still on earth because they would like to enjoy the benefits of material life without restraint. They are materialists in the truest sense of the word, who only wished to return to earth because they consider it the pinnacle of existence.

As I have already said, they will have to experience bitter disappointments until such time as they find the right path to spiritual progress.

It is different for people who come to earth with a progressive programme, but do not find the right way immediately on account of their materialistic environment. They suffer from the conflict. And it depends on the power of their free will and the condition and strength of their souls whether they can struggle through and reach their goals. A person who returns to earth with good intentions and the desire to make spiritual progress discovers very soon, or better said, soon doubts, whether the mundane outlook of life, which his surroundings impose upon him, come up to his expectations. He will examine the matter from all sides, weigh the results and true benefits and look for a way which is compatible with the blueprint he has brought with him.

But one must bear in mind that a person has no possibility of assessing his own spiritual standard and therefore looks for somebody whom he considers an ideal human being in the belief that people who have lived longer must have better knowledge and more experience. This should be the case, but it is not, because people do not have the same stage of development and are at quite dissimilar degrees of spiritual maturity.

Therefore, it is very difficult for individuals to know not only whether they are on the right course of life, but also which actually is the right one and where they will obtain information about it.

This brings me to the subject of self-education. Only people who earnestly wish to make progress, not material progress, and aspire to develop their personalities will scrutinise themselves closely and criticise their way of life and their attitude to their surroundings.

But this too gives rise to questions that are not always easy to answer and sometimes cannot be answered at all. It is a very serious problem. I have already said that one has to be able to understand and forgive oneself. When the stage has been reached that a person endeavours to understand his own behaviour, then he will soon be able to judge whether his opinion of himself is honest and unprejudiced. Only then is it of value. To lie to oneself is pointless, but equally, unwarranted criticism is wrong.

How can a person know if he has a correct opinion about himself and whether he has judged his behaviour correctly? Everybody has his conscience, his inner voice and therefore his spiritual leader whom he should, and can, trust in every situation in life. This knowledge must gain an ever-increasing place in the life of every individual. "A quiet conscience sleeps in thunder" is no empty phrase. It is truly so, except that what one calls a "conscience" is one's guiding spirit. Everybody has one at his side who, questioned sincerely and with goodwill, will always give the correct answer.

In the world beyond it is substantially easier, because there the person sees his guide or guides and helpers. It is left to his discretion to trust their leadership and follow their good advice.

As so much has already been written and spoken about this in earthly life and the Church also demands that people examine their conscience and speaks of a guardian angel, I am prompted to deal with this subject truthfully and explain it, so that the right path can easily be found.

The earthly interpretation of conscience is that it is nothing other than self-criticism, therefore it is a purely intellectual occurrence, an activity of the brain. The truth is that the soul is receptive to the influence and advice of its guide and welcomes the judgement and counsel with cheerful consent.

Goodwill stems from the spirit entity and stimulates receptiveness, the crowning spiritual achievement in the life of a material person.

We do not prize this achievement so highly because we know our good, benevolent, and often very strict guides and can easily communicate with them in a recognisable way.

But this is the wise, divine dispensation of Providence, that earthly man is forced to acquire contact by his own efforts and must fulfil and master the tasks set for him without visible guidance or compulsion. It is a very serious and arduous undertaking, particularly when the true correlations are not known. How much easier it would be for a person to receive a conscious answer from the universe, instead of relying on a decision or a line of argument which could stem from misunderstanding his own thoughts.

Therefore to educate oneself means, in the first instance, to entrust oneself to one's spiritual guide and heed his advice and warnings. But this should not be too broadly interpreted. A person should not try to establish in this way whether a purely material project is going to succeed or not. Only spiritual questions should be asked when an attitude towards fellow men is to be considered or if one's own character and self-estimation is under examination.

This last question is most important. One should put it to one's guide time and again. It is extremely valuable and encompasses everything that affects character and personality – therefore the spirit entity. There must be no doubt as to whether a good deed was spontaneous or calculated, and whether one's estimation of a person was correct or wrong. Deep within himself everybody finds the answer which his guide has given him.

If inner excitement or outside disturbances prevent the body from attaining the relaxation necessary to make spiritual contact with one's guide, then, as people say, one should simply sleep on it. After a good night's rest the answer is obvious.

For while man is asleep, his good, spiritual guide is at work giving the poor, erring earthling security, peace and strength of purpose. Everybody should acknowledge him as his master. He certainly deserves the fullest confidence and thanks.

Self-education is faith in all positive powers and the strong will to reject all those that are negative.

The purpose and goal of self-education differs from person to person. Deep inside everybody feels in how far it is necessary to reorientate himself.

Self-education presupposes the absolute will to achieve the personification of an ideal if not in every respect, then at least in those areas that affect relationships with people around us, and *vice versa*.

One of the main tasks of earthly existence is to practise patience. Patience with oneself and with one's fellow men, and this because we know that everyone suffers from the mistakes he makes. This suffering continues until knowledge dawns. We demand patience from those around us and must give it in the measure we would receive it.

To practise patience also means to grant and receive help at the same time in the endeavour to get closer to the truth, to Divinity, for everything true is irrefutably correct and good. What is not true is evil. Even if it is not so in the final consequence, it is the error which impedes progress.

Additionally, to practise patience with oneself is the second requirement of self-education. With the best will in the world, the erring, ignorant person is often not able to readjust his way of thinking and acting as he would like and as he sees he ought to.

Patience with those around us is a basis for kindness and good deeds. When once one reaches this stage, progress can no longer be impeded.

I still owe an explanation. I said before that we should practise patience. The "we" was deliberate, because the principle for self-education applies to all of us whether we are on earth or in the world beyond. But the way it happens in the world beyond is different. It is difficult to compare it with the process on earth since the material body and organs, which permit the act of thinking and the implementation of deeds, is lacking. It is better not to probe too deeply into this area. As I have often mentioned, the expressions and concepts which would avoid misleading comparisons do not exist in earthly language.

As far as the spirit is concerned, the requirements and principles are the same in both worlds. The process is different, but the goal we strive towards is always the same.

We will leave it at that and close with both the feeling and the reflection that everything flows towards the goal – the peaceful, divine harbour – in a common stream.

Be assured that nobody is excluded from this wonderful progression, no matter how great and difficult the obstacles to be surmounted. This may serve to put the purpose of self-education into a proper light and underline the value of an existence that should only advance development. The tasks are serious and laborious, but as I have said repeatedly, the effort will be rewarded. I am able to say this. I speak from experience.

Suggestion and auto-suggestion.
Submission through free will and opposition.

YESTERDAY we wrote about self-education and the necessary thoughts for this.

Only thought, the power of thought, which we have already discussed elsewhere, can have either a good or bad influence on the development of a character – a personality. Thoughts can also be generated by outside influences, by wrong examples or through the thoughts of others, which trigger a corresponding reaction in one's own thinking.

I have already said that bad thoughts affect one's fellow men and can harm their souls.

How often is a child intimidated and uncertain because it feels the thoughts of its parents, who are often unnecessarily concerned that their children should behave properly. Properly of course, according to their standards. They just wait for the child to misbehave and discredit them. The child will immediately falter and realise their fears. We will have more to say about this.

I also spoke about the fact that one's own thoughts have an even greater power on oneself. One smiles a little at the idea of suggestion and auto-suggestion, usually if one isn't quite sure what they mean, and how this power can be used.

Auto-suggestion is easier than telepathy. One is always receptive to one's own thoughts. In the case of telepathy the recipient must be prepared to accept the transferred thought if, for example, a certain act is to be brought about in this way.

The effect of thoughts on others is not quite suggestion, although it is the beginning of it. Suggestion is transference of thought and will. It is an influence, to be more precise, a conscious influence of the free will of someone else with particular intentions towards the person in question.

If two people are in harmony, the will of one will always adapt to that of the other, or may even be subordinate to it.

If somebody does not have the power to withstand the will – the bad will – of another, he becomes an abulic tool, as the saying goes. This is far removed from harmony, which occurs not only with personal will but with very much good will.

Principally, I want to talk about auto-suggestion, because it will play an important role in self-education. It is the ability to free oneself from negative influences and thoughts, to introduce a mental state which is a step – even a small one – towards an ideal human character.

People who are aware of the power and might of their thoughts can use them in an undreamed of manner to progress in all areas of spiritual and material life.

Of course, the power of thought should only be used to further progress, to intensify vital energy. If this has been diminished and harmed through unfavourable influences, it should be used to restore it.

Let us take a concrete illustration. If a person has been weakened by a severe illness and no medicine can replace the strength that has been lost, then positive thought, and a positive attitude towards favourable influences coupled with a rejection of all negative manifestations, will re-charge his strength to a degree that will amaze many a doctor. This is why one speaks of a sick person's strong will to live. Subconscious auto-suggestion is at work with thoughts like, "I am definitely not going to die. I do not want to. I must get well. I must still fulfil this or that task," and so on. Miracles, from the human point of view, do not only occur in such extreme cases. Much good can also be achieved in daily life in this way.

The little words "I must" and "I will" and "There is no obstacle that I cannot overcome" serve to make every undertaking a success in advance, however impossible it appears at first. Of course, the undertaking has to be feasible. The best resolve and the strongest auto-suggestion will not alter the fact that a person cannot lift a thousand kilos on his own. Also, it must not contradict the eternal laws of nature. Above all, sound guidance of thoughts will help to achieve that in the case of an unusual undertaking – say that of an artist who has to perform in front of a large audience – he will be freed once and for all of inhibitions and stage fright. This is really progress, because these negative feelings are born of fear of human censure.

Total success is only possible if one has confidence in oneself, if one is self-assured and consequently allows one's own powers, knowledge and ability free reign. How often does an examinee fail because, in spite of the knowledge he has gained through study, he feels he is not in full command of the subject.

In my medical practice, I have freed many a soul of fear, thereby helping him to success. How much easier it will be when people are completely convinced that this aspect of material life is unimportant; that the value and the maturity of a human being is shown in ways other than examinations of academic knowledge learned by heart.

But I do not wish to dwell on this. I want to talk about the art of self-education, which will not only bring about progress in the spirit sense, but also in the material sense in the mastery of tasks that have nothing to do with spiritual progress.

I must stress that it is the duty of parents to instil into their children a sense of self-education. Alone the faith that one shows in allowing them to decide themselves on their course of action engenders great self-confidence. This is enormous progress in the development of a young person. But more particularly it generates increased trust in the parents, who do not only force the child by orders and punishment to have the correct attitude towards life and its obligations. In this way they best become the confidants and friends of their children, who will turn to them should they be unable to make the correct decision in matters of life themselves.

Now let us examine something else – opposition. This is the endeavour to enforce one's own will if outside pressure tries to prevent the realisation of an undertaking.

Opposition is neither a disallowed nor a culpable conduct. It is, so to say, the normal reaction to attack. It comes to the fore when the spirit entity and above all the soul is not prepared to obey a command and to subordinate itself to a foreign will.

I have already said that souls in harmony gladly subordinate themselves to each other, but that spirit entities with very dissimilar radiations and different degrees of maturity will find it extremely difficult to act in concord. Of course, the degrees of opposition and their consequences might vary considerably. No two people will offer opposition in the same way and with the same intensity, even though they make the impression of being similar.

Above all, one must distinguish between opposition to a harmful attack and one to a well-meant action. A person who endeavours to develop only in a good sense will probably often feel an internal opposition, an opposition in his thoughts, to good advice or to interference in accordance with human social order which encroaches upon his personal freedom. However his spirit, striving to progress, will recognise the benefit of such constraint and immediately submit freely to it. Such an attitude is correct and beneficial.

It is a different matter if the opposition forces one to do the opposite of what is requested and one does not react because one realises that one will not succeed against the person making demands. Such submission is without free will; it is by reason of common sense, which does not acknowledge the dictate, but does so because it is more convenient.

This type of forced obedience, which is demanded in every stage of life, is unhealthy. It is insincere and causes an accumulation of thoughts and feelings which prompt a person into opposition. It usually comes to a head when the opportunity occurs, but it is not appropriate for the personal will to become operative.

People who in their childhood were well-behaved and obedient, to the eminent satisfaction of their parents, often become aware all of a sudden of their free will and realise that essentially they also have the right and the ability to make decisions. They reach a point where they want to impose their will on everything, for as it has been suppressed so long it usually overreacts. People in this situation are badly off and make many mistakes.

The time must come when parents learn to guide the free will of the child instead of trying to enforce their own will through punishment, prohibition and orders. This is a big mistake.

It is not only in the education of a child that we can see this opposition, which is the result of constraint. In every human social order there are regulations, restrictions, prohibitions and penalties which provoke protest to a greater or lesser extent among society or the state in question. Here too the point must be reached where people of their own free will think and want to do only what is good, helpful and advantageous for society.

In the chapter on penal law, I spoke about the fact that through compulsion and punishment no improvement would be obtained in a misguided or erring mind; that the will to find the right way would have to be awakened in a different manner.

The greatest degree of opposition is produced by punishment. Instead of improvement it only leads to the most intense aversion to human society. No criminal considers punishment justifiable. His innermost feeling tells him that this is not what will bring home to him the wickedness or wrongness of his deed. What *will* is his inner voice, his conscience, his good leader whom he does not listen to. When he realises this, his spiritual progress has begun. He would like to make good his error; he wishes it had never happened, that he had never committed the evil deed. Through punishment he is forced into a state of opposition, whether he wants it or not. From this develops a hatred for jurisdiction, and yes, for the entire human social order.

Do finally realise that in this way there can be no progress for humanity, and have the courage to make a clean sweep of this incorrect view of punishment, atonement and its supposed consequences of improvement.

Opposition in politics is another matter. In the main it stems from bad will or from a need for personal recognition and is always unhealthy. In this area people must learn that only unanimous, selfless co-operation brings real success; that the individual is so insignificant in the huge universe with its regular course of time and events and that the community cannot benefit from opposition, but only from achievements reached in co-operation.

Today the enormous differences are still due to the overrating of material possessions, because only these cause class and social barriers in human life instead of a system based on spiritual maturity in the true sense of the word.

In my work, I often had the opportunity to study this incorrect classification in matters of human values. I looked for – and if I may say so, found – a different standard.

Why should not such a point of view, which today I know is the totally correct one, become general knowledge? In the not too distant future it will be so, when people realise that spirituality is not on a par with material blessings, but is quite independent of wealth.

When considering the personality of people, strip them of all their material riches and visible trappings. Look inside them. Examine only the maturity of their spirit and soul, then you will classify them correctly and the knowledge of human nature will have a different meaning to what is has today. The next time we will think about this.

Knowledge of human nature
and its practical application.

WITH spiritual eyes I see things quite differently from material people. I see what they do incorrectly and how wrongly they think. It is this that I want to talk about.

I will gear my comments to earthly sight, so that I am not tempted to confound the spiritual with the material, which would lead to total confusion.

Knowledge of human nature means to know the character of your fellow men. The expression is obvious. But we do not want to begin at the end. We want to point out what is necessary in order to attain the correct knowledge of human nature.

How will we judge another person and know how to estimate his value if we have not studied ourselves and judged ourselves down to the last detail? This is the first big mistake we make.

Knowledge of human nature – and I use this term in the earthly sense as the endeavour to identify human behaviour patterns and character traits and not as knowledge that has already been acquired – is based on the assumption that you know and have examined yourself very thoroughly, and are able to establish if you can be considered an ideal type of a person – a prototype against which you can measure other people.

What are you actually hoping to achieve? One often says, and this concept is widespread, that knowledge of human nature is the most important aspect of one's relations with one's fellow men. In the main this is correct, but it is not as important as is generally supposed.

In order to pass judgement on the actions and the character of a person and to avoid any mistake, you would need spiritual eyes. The material body does not allow a view of the inner being of people. Therefore, a judgement beyond all shadow of a doubt is never possible.

But as we should only judge according to water-tight knowledge and evidence, we have to pass up this approach in our search for knowledge of human nature.

The impression that everybody has of his fellow men is one that he creates according to his own spiritual maturity, so that everybody will have a different impression of the same person, although the principal characteristics will be more or less the same.

Nevertheless, in human life it is necessary to have as accurate as possible a picture of the people around us. It can more or less approximate to the truth; geared to particular abilities and characteristics, it can be correct and point the way to human contact and co-operation, but one will never be able to receive a perfectly accurate overall impression of character.

It also depends which radiations emanate from two people at such an examination; whether there is a feeling of harmony or a need to keep one's distance.

An objective impression is not possible because every examination of this kind is subjective. But the doctor requires just such an objective impression for his character analysis and tries to obtain it by a scientific system which analyses impulses and behaviour. These results he abstracts and compares with universal scientific findings.

The goodwill and the commendable intention is certainly to be applauded. It is a modest beginning, to which I wish to add my comments in order to lend this unpretentious foundation some weight and make it the basis for more advanced and successful research work. I have already mentioned that everybody is a unique individual, that no two spirit entities in the world are alike, at least not in the spheres that we are in a position to take into account.

On the physical plane nobody embodies the ideal; there is no one whom everybody should attempt to model himself on. But there are characteristic features in earthly life, situations and circumstances that are valid for everybody. But if a person only achieves success in a limited portion of these combined circumstances, or in any human relations, the conclusion should not be drawn that he is unable to do justice to all the requirements of human society, which is to say that he is lacking in this respect.

Of course, there are demands which I have not included here. These are the obvious demands of civilisation and culture, but they are areas of life which everybody has to choose and which underline and form a personal character. They are independent of the community as a whole and are left to the free will of every individual.

Individual psychology has established three areas which point the way to knowledge of human nature: marriage, career and friendship. After what I have said in previous chapters I can only repeat that this classification is based on the great error which still has such an inhibitory effect on science today. This is the assumption that man comes only once to earth and therefore has to strive to acquire all the attributes of an ideal person in accordance with the material concept of life.

How often, after careful study, have we succeeded in finding such a person? Perhaps more frequently than we care to admit, but in many cases we have been wide of the mark.

It is not easy for us to make a really objective decision about a person. The value of a character depends on so many things. Just think how many people appear to be good, simply because they never have the opportunity to show us their unpleasant side. How often do we experience that people, who as children were constantly protected and kept away from all supposedly bad influences, fail completely in later life when all protection falls away and they are suddenly confronted with the seriousness of existence. They allow their base instincts and desires free reign and have not the slightest wish to return to a well-ordered lifestyle.

As long as a person is subordinate to outside influences, or the barriers imposed upon him by his surroundings have not been removed, it will be difficult to fathom the latent potential traits in his character. It is, of course, correct that individual psychology concentrates its examination on those fields of human life which play the greatest role in human society or those which are not to be separated in their correlations from the human community.

Marriage is the bond which maintains mankind on earth; it is the basis for its procreation and preservation. This cannot be denied, and in accordance with the dictates of civilisation the institution, as established by law, must be acknowledged as such. But why should a person who does not contract matrimony and has no part in the procreation and maintenance of man in this lifetime be of less value than one, who although he obeys the dictates of marriage, nevertheless does not do mankind a big service? I have already said that the ideal person cannot be sought and formed in one lifetime, and in the earthly sense does not exist.

But if we proceed on the assumption that man will one day have reached such a state of maturity that everything bad and ugly disappears, then we can speak of a person who is tantamount to ideal in the earthly sense.

Today's requirements are mainly targeted towards material success. Man does not know the real reason for his various existences.

But now it is necessary to learn to define the boundaries allocated to everybody for his life on earth, and recognise the areas in which he must make progress.

Knowledge of human nature does not mean to establish whether a person conforms to the demands of civilisation and community life. If, for example, he is not inclined to marry, it may be a benefit, even a blessing for mankind. To push him into marriage is quite wrong. The interference of outsiders is neither good nor necessary because no harm is done and the personality is not damaged if earthly marriage is not contracted. To impose pressure in this matter is a great mistake.

Mothers must learn that not every woman is destined to bear children or serve a man. Life offers so many opportunities to develop motherly qualities. It is often unmarried women who display talents that many a mother would be happy to possess.

Do not create an inferiority complex in people through the mistaken concept of placing a mother above an unmarried woman. Rather try to establish in which direction her work for this life lies and clear the obstacles from her path which prevent her from fulfilling the task she has taken on herself.

A way must be found to recognise the course of life of every person, the abilities that have been given him and the spiritual maturity already achieved. Then one will see the obstacles that stand in the way of free development; in how far a greater maturity of spirit is necessary to succeed, or how the environment must be changed, or actually created as a basis for such achievements.

A person who has a career that has been forced on him by his family, one that totally contradicts the abilities he has brought with him, will be dissatisfied and unhappy until he has been helped out of the impasse or has found his true calling, which could be a secondary occupation.

Often a person lacks the courage to renounce the path onto which he has been guided and turn against the will of his family. Here medical or psychological care must intervene.

It is not blind obedience that must be requested, but courageous embarkation on the self-chosen course of life. Nobody can claim the right to pave the way for somebody else, or better said, to prescribe the course of life for another without having examined this person thoroughly and correctly. This no earthly person can do. One may assist an individual to prepare a chosen course of life and help to remove obstacles of whatever kind, but one may never exert pressure against the free will of a person in matters that are so important and significant for his progress. Not even when, in the opinion of "cleverer people" the right path has been missed, or brings no material benefit.

These are the fundamental ideas about knowledge of human nature which should not be only theoretical phrases and mere awareness, but practical help on the upward path; a helping hand for the mastery of all human problems.

Everybody has the right to choose his own path. It is the concern of his fellow men – particularly doctors and priests – to recognise and remove the material obstacles. We will identify and discuss these obstacles individually. Their identification will be a practical way of getting to know human nature.

And here we have reached the point from which we must proceed if we wish to provide a suitable concept, which could be a base for this practical knowledge of human nature.

As I have already said, as far as a correct and sound philosophy of life is concerned, mankind is still in its infancy. It cannot mature as long as it will not, or dare not, look beyond the limited horizon of materialism. It will not, because material pleasures prevent it from doing so and the fear to have to forego them is very real; and it dare not, because the Church forbids it. Only in very exceptional cases is the right path found.

One can easily imagine how great the difficulties are when contrary to all expectations and logical – but material – reasoning, a child displays abilities and qualities other than those which are the norm in its family. If it is a spirit that towers above these people, the greatest confusion can arise, because no explanation can be found for its behaviour. Or it creates bitter disappointment, because in spite of all the trouble that has been taken, the child cannot attain the standard of its siblings.

Fundamentally the principle must be accepted that spiritual characteristics are not inherited. There is only an extrinsic influence from the environment – parents, profession, friends and so on. These influences are what one has to watch out for and recognise. It depends on the strength of the soul, which is exposed to them and on its power, either to dismiss or to accept and adopt them.

The difficulties for the investigating psychologist are obvious. How often is one inclined to regard a characteristic of a person as being his own, whereas it has only been instilled and is not an inherent part of the personality. To distinguish between the two and decide what is a characteristic trait and what has been instilled is very difficult. In many cases, it is impossible.

It is easier to establish the personality when a person is older, as influence, upbringing and so on are no longer so effective and his own judgement has matured from experience. This is why one so seldom finds a young person who is sure of himself and acts with confidence. The outside influences – the criticism, and the often extremely anxious expectation of his family – inhibit and restrict his free will.

When once the stage is reached that one accepts that every newborn child comes equipped with a complete blueprint and this is left free reign, so that the superiority of the adult towards the child melts like snow in the sun, then one will stand like an explorer at the cradle of the baby and endeavour to give its free will unlimited possibilities to express itself.

The correct philosophy of life would be a milestone on the way to the right knowledge of human nature and show a higher commitment which would have pride of place in a person's education.

Next time I will discuss the errors committed as a result of a totally material philosophy of life and how one should counter them, even without believing in eternal and ever-recurring life on earth.

Errors which occur during the
investigation of human character.
The influence of a previous life on the
development of earthly life.

TODAY I am going to point out how a material philosophy of life can lead to errors in the study of the character and the abilities of people.

The effort to help individuals to succeed in their battles in life has certainly been made and developed to a science which, although still in its infancy, is a suitable basis for future construction and progress. The big mistake made – as already stated – is that to a certain degree one tends to measure everything with the same yardstick.

But as we have heard, no two people have the same goal in life, and the way to a supposedly common goal is different for everybody. Obstructions and difficulties have to be prepared for one person; for another, the path to progress is smooth.

Who can decide and recognise this? Certainly not material man with his limited horizon and his inability to regress further than birth.

In the material sphere the greatest care is required to find the correct method for everybody in need of help.

The soul, this delicate instrument which in the first instance is reserved for the spirit entity to play upon, requires very circumspect treatment from without and care, not to be confused with care of the body, which is the psychologist's main and most fascinating task. It does not make sense to remain at the point which our forbears and teachers reached in their knowledge. I am able to reveal that today they all recognise the mistakes they made and would dearly like to instruct people in the way I have been allowed to. Look upon me as their spokesman. Believe me, we have all agreed on what we consider was correct and what was mistaken in our teachers' instructions.

I must always repeat that the main reason for these mistakes in the material philosophy of life is the belief that there is only one life on this earth for people. This view will never lead to a correct assessment of soul and spirit. At the most, by comparison with others, one can establish which general abilities and fundamentals are present, how the influences of the outside world affect people, what traits they have in common and which influences are either good or bad.

I have already said that some influences which observers would consider negative can be part of a person's life picture. His task during his sojourn on earth is to master and overcome them. Everybody should be in the position to find the power to do this without outside help. And this assistance would not be necessary if it were not for purely material disturbances like an inherited physical inferiority or a weakness which prevents the inherent power from becoming sufficiently effective.

And here doctors and human society must make an effort to recognise which difficulties are to be overcome. These are not only material and environmental, but also emotional and mental caused by the immature development of the spirit entity and the soul.

It is not easy for me to think myself into the earthly perceptive faculty of scholars and accept as a basis for scientific research what is assumed as fact according to the material viewpoint. To have a perfect and really successful knowledge of human nature, it is necessary to possess an insight into the past, into the stages of life that have already been completed, or conversely, knowledge of human nature which is always a patchwork affair for material man. It requires a particular ability to distinguish between a person's inherent and extrinsic emotions.

Positive emotions, also those instilled and acquired only in earthly life, need not be examined. It is different with mistakes which the soul does not have the power to resist.

Results in the education of people must therefore be very dissimilar. It is mainly a question of assessing the individual. For this common guidelines can be drawn up and used.

But one person cannot be judged by comparing him with another. As I have said, it is no disadvantage if a spirit entity demonstrates one-sided abilities because nobody knows how far other fields have been mastered in a previous existence.

Other mistakes play a role here. Marriage, for example, which in the material world is considered the absolute and most desirable goal for every healthy and normal person, seldom fulfils the expectations attached to it. Fulfilment in the truest sense of the word is only possible if it is made in heaven. This means if it is the meeting of two souls who complement each other as twin souls. I have already pointed out that no spirit entity can attain perfection on his own, that for this he must find his complement who was destined for him from the beginning. I would say it is written in the stars when the spirit entities destined for each other are allowed to unite. There is no set rule for this, but the time for such a union is determined according to the infinite laws of nature.

The material matrimonial bond is therefore not left to peoples' whims. It is simply a union to ensure the procreation and preservation of mankind. The "preservation of mankind" means the preservation of the foundations which give the spirit entity, who wishes to return to earth, the necessary and suitable conditions for his earthly existence. A marriage without procreation is not a marriage in a higher sense. At the most, in the opinion of the world beyond, it is a comradely or friendly association.

The earthly interpretation of marriage is that it is the gratification of sensual love or desire. It has little or nothing at all to do with the harmony of the two souls in question.

The Church has made a heavenly institution of marriage which is incorrect because in the world beyond there are no sexes; the material bodies are lacking. Nevertheless it is, also in earthly existence, an institution which signifies a commitment between partners. Obligations, undertaken with an oath of fidelity and loyalty, must be fulfilled. Of course, this is easily said. Mistakes are made here too and people are not always strong enough and so committed to the oath that they are aware of their great responsibility and in a position to reach, by hook or by crook, the end of the road they have embarked upon. In this area mankind still errs to a great extent.

As already indicated, it is only rarely possible to recognise the real character of a person. Often he only shows his true colours when the barriers, which the environment frequently imposes on a young person, fall away. But then, on account of fear of censure from fellow men, or simply because the courage or strength is lacking, the unhappy partner thinks everything has to be endured and does not even consider the thought of a separation. So very many reflections and opinions are justified in this respect, for no two marriages are alike.

One can, for example, by no means make the rule that a marriage, in which harmony of souls is lacking, should be terminated. Nobody should judge such a matter, but instead ought to, in as helpful a manner as possible, smooth the way which a disappointed person is willing to take. This is the duty of the community. Criticism is never correct because it is without exact knowledge of the actual circumstances. This is why knowledge of human nature can never be based on a rigid pattern, but should rather follow the line of intuitive understanding, geared to the person in question.

The diversity of characters and the divergence of spiritual maturity, caused by the infinite laws, require as many ways of looking at things as there are people. One cannot say that a person who has a reasonable mastery of marriage, friendship and career embodies the ideal. What is reasonable mastery? There can be no answer to this. The very fact that a marriage has produced so and so many children and in the eyes of the world is conducted in perfect harmony is certainly not the correct standard by which it should be judged. This is only possible in the spiritual aspect, and a material person can only pass judgement to a limited degree. Enough for today.

One-sided development. Career and calling.

YESTERDAY we spoke about the fact that people are really not capable of studying human nature the way it should be done. As long as one is not in a position to recognise and control the spiritual influences from extra-terrestrial spheres, it must be an incomplete, patchwork affair.

Nevertheless, the beginnings that have been made are good to a certain extent and have shown that what has been achieved so far has alleviated much harm that has occurred to the soul. Knowledge of human nature infers the understanding which we have already discussed. Understanding is the basis for successful help.

The study of human nature ought not to be pursued only for the sake of science. It should serve progress, both one's own and that of the community. One's own, because in understanding the conduct of one's fellow men one will be able to enjoy the company of others and be ready to help them, which after all must be the chief quality of an advanced spirit. As I have already said, the doctrines which apply today to the knowledge of human nature are based on the assumption that in this life everything must be achieved that constitutes a perfect person, one who is held in highest esteem in human society.

We have spoken about marriage and its purpose and in this context established that it is by no means necessary for every good, advanced spirit to fulfil nature's laws; it is not known whether perhaps in an earlier life extraordinary maturity may have been achieved in this regard, so that in the current life the main emphasis lies in other directions which will advance progress.

Because, I repeat once again, it is a ridiculous concept that man should have to embody in one life on earth all that is possible and desirable for society. Nobody is capable of doing this.

To be sure, individual psychology already knows this and has acknowledged that people do justice to one or two of the three requirements, and to what extent. It is a standard for the assessment, the necessary treatments and the instruction, which everybody supposedly needs, in order to be closer to the so-called ideal type. One is already satisfied if a person succeeds moderately in every area, but one condemns one-sidedness. That is not right.

How often are women considered abnormal or under-developed because they are not suited to marriage; because they have no sensual desire for men and do not even have the need for such desire. On the contrary, they are often the more highly developed and mature spirit entities because they outgrew sensual love in an earlier life when they recognised its negligible value. Their motherliness does not have to go to waste because of this. It has absolutely nothing to do with sensual love.

Material difficulties are probably often the reason that people refuse to have children. They do not know and cannot divine that the infinite laws have established set rules in this respect too.

To violate nature's laws and prevent births is a mistake; more than that, it is a crime if it is done not out of concern for the yet unborn, perhaps poor, sick child, but out of personal convenience and possibly for material-financial reasons and greed. I will write about this on another occasion.

Therefore, do not force a daughter into marriage. Wedlock does not always benefit mankind. And do not automatically condemn as abnormal and unnatural a woman or man who is unmarried.

And now, the profession. This is an important and tricky subject for me, because from here I only see and can only acknowledge a career which at the same time is a calling.

In earthly existence there are many professions and occupations which have nothing to do with a calling and only enable a person to exist in the purely material sense. It is very important to recognise this difference when judging a human character, spiritual maturity and the personality as such.

That a person is successful and makes great progress in work that he has selected, or which has been forced on him, is by no means the proof that he has chosen the right career even when people believe it to be so if they amass material goods and are rich and independent. "I have found my right niche" is the verdict of everybody who is able to go through life without worries. But when such a person is old and no longer in a position to acquire more riches, he is dissatisfied because his entire happiness has been based on the acquisition of goods and riches and not – and this is true in most cases – in their proper exploitation, as ordained by God. Then the success of his life seems small and unimportant, and he realises that what he has called his career has been a useless occupation. But then it is too late. A career which does not offer a person the possibility of working for the community and doing a good job is not a calling, and in the sense of spiritual progress can only be considered a sideline.

A calling is the most valuable gift of Heaven, a favour which everybody who is aware of the urge that must be fulfiled within him should be eternally grateful for. As I have already said, it cannot be acquired or obtained by force; it must be earned by good deeds.

Later I will write more about this, but now to round off the subject I want to add what I consider important. A career which does not promote spiritual progress because it is purely material cannot satisfy anybody. But there are few such careers. They are those which have been established to the detriment of human society and only gratify the exaggerated material pleasures without creating beauty or harmony. Practically all other professions give rise to the feeling of the necessity of the occupation and, coupled with the proper philosophy of life, give people satisfaction and inner peace.

Work done only for the material benefits and income is without value for spiritual progress, no matter how progressive it may seem.

I want to make it quite clear that it is necessary to know whether one's work gives happiness and satisfaction.

If this is not the case, then it is time to choose a spare-time occupation which does. This is already well known. The discontent of the masses can be traced to the fact that people find no inner satisfaction in their work. Unless they have a second occupation in some other field, they begin to compare themselves with other people and blame all the disadvantages of their own lives on their demanding careers. They certainly do not want to realise that the cause lies within themselves.

Therefore, it is the duty of those who concern themselves with the study of personality, the knowledge of human nature, to help such erring little sheep onto the right path and assist them to find an occupation which will serve to aid the people around them – the community – but at the same time benefits them in their own progress, in the development of their intelligence and the enrichment of their knowledge.

The progress of the individual, even without consequences for the community, is of great value. It is the basis for a later life, and often the prerequisite for a calling, a duty given by the grace of God.

Therefore, it is not as easy as one thinks to judge whether a person can cope with his career, and, in the opinion of the individual psychologist, fulfils the requirements of an ideal type of person. Up till now one has been inclined to consider material success the yardstick; one has often discovered and been amazed to realise that despite such material success people are highly dissatisfied and discontented. One was inclined to look for the reason in other areas and to say that it could not be the career. Perhaps the marriage was not quite in order, or friendships had been neglected on account of the demanding profession. This is usually not the case. The answer is quite simply that the career, which man considers all-important, was not properly chosen and the necessary compensation, which a better and more successful secondary occupation would have given, was lacking.

When judging a personality it must therefore first be established if his career is fulfilling and to what extent. According to the degree of satisfaction, and this is not established by what the person in question says, but exemplified by his way of life, one may then assess his personality. So much for today. Tomorrow we will speak about friendship.

True friendship and its basic conditions.

TODAY we will speak about friendship, how individual psychology defines it and what it really is.

People are not too particular about using the term "friend." If a person seems well disposed towards them they are quick to call him a friend. If, in addition, he does them a favour, the friendship is sealed.

But if one works scientifically with such notions, it is not so simple. One can have confidence in a person. One can think highly of him and respect him. All dealings with him may have proved extremely satisfactory. But he is still not to be called a friend.

In the first instance, friendship demands reciprocity of feelings and judgement of each other. Friendship means a high degree of harmony, perhaps more than is necessary in wedlock, because marriage can also exist if harmony is absent or only present to a limited degree.

If harmony, the unison of souls, is lacking between friends, then it is no friendship, or the friendship is past. This also is hardly possible, because true friendship lasts beyond the grave, and nothing or nobody can disturb it. Therefore a friendship that is over, is only a delusion, a mistake and, depending on the degree of cooling off, is more – or less – tragic. However a disappointment need not necessarily lead to an immediate break-up.

There are very few people who have the ability to be friends. Up to now individual psychology has considered the term in relation to the attitude towards the community; the more – or less – strongly developed ability to be social and friendly with people, to help them or to have the desire to give them pleasure. But this is by no means sufficient for the real designation of friendship.

In my medical practice I used to ask patients if they had a friend. For the most part I received the reply that such a person could not be found; there were good acquaintances, but there was more to expect from a friend. And this is quite true.

But because true friendship is so rare, it should not be concluded that there is no sense in looking for such a person, or to trust anybody at all. On the contrary, it should prove a stimulation that one is capable of being a true friend to another person. This means to harmonise with him in all matters, to understand all his actions, to vouch for him in all situations in life and to make all sacrifices for him.

Of course; this does not mean that he should be given support in incorrect dealings and objectively unacceptable situations. In this case it is a matter of counselling and giving the erring friend advice; helping him unselfishly to find the right path without condemning him. This is certainly not always easy. It belongs to the theme of all-embracing love.

Friendship demands the dedication of the whole personality with no egoistical ulterior motives. Conviviality is very good for people, but not everybody has the ability to fraternise, and even if, fundamentally, the qualities which allow social intercourse exist, the influences of the surroundings are mainly the reason that people isolate themselves or do not have the courage to take part in jovial gatherings. But it is also not easy to find the company that the spirit needs for entertainment and relaxation.

Emptiness, triviality, and banality are often the basis of social gatherings. Hardly anybody goes home enriched from such meetings unless they have brought him material advantages. People whose souls are in tune and who are not too far apart in spiritual maturity should get together. It is immaterial whether they belong to a higher or lower level of the social order. Harmony between souls and spirit entities can be recognised by attitude and in the earthly sphere by their aura, which we here see quite clearly and unmistakably.

Matter serves only to give people the possibility of doing the right thing through free will, without influence or visible guidance; to strive for success in earthly life in order to know the limits within which the results achieved may be enjoyed.

But now back to our subject, friendship. Do not indiscriminately call everybody who appeals to you at first glance a friend! It damages the interpretation of this important relationship in human society. Have as many good acquaintances as you like, but only one friend if you have been granted the luck to find him in this life on earth.

The attitude to establish a friendship between two people must be carefully studied and considered. The prerequisite is total honesty. Between friends there must be no lies and no withholding of information, which is tantamount to a lie. Keeping quiet is only permitted if it is about matters like bodily defects or shortcomings among the people around him, which could cause him pain. Honesty must not go so far as to tell the truth at all costs.

A considered, considerate silence can often be beneficial and delightful. It incorporates an understanding and a forgiveness that often works wonders and bestows a strength that no spoken word can engender so impressively. To be quiet at the right time is often very important in a friendship, because we have already heard that no two people are alike and therefore differences can occur in many a point of view.

Great insight is necessary in order to understand correctly, because everybody is inclined to judge matters from his own level, from his own experience and from his own visual faculty.

How often does one realise in retrospect that a situation, which led to a particular line of action, was quite different from the way it had been understood, because the moment the other person began to speak one's own ideas began to form and paint a picture. How dissimilar are the pictures that result.

Insight into the thoughts of others is a necessity in every situation in life if one does not want to make mistakes at every turn and come to the wrong conclusion about associates. To this must be added the ability to adapt oneself to the person, the will and the wishes of another. Insight is the striving to understand, to recognise correctly and to adjust one's line of action accordingly.

The ability to adapt oneself is the subordination of one's own will to that of one's friend. But there must be a very clear distinction between adaption and subservience. If adaption goes to the point where one's own will is totally eliminated, then one surrenders completely to the will of the other person and becomes an abulic tool. This cannot be the sense and the purpose of friendship.

To show insight is to conform to the will of another, simply because, on consideration, his will has been properly expressed and there is no reason to contradict it.

In friendship one person cannot be superior to the other. Unanimity, that is, the wish to agree, should always be easily achieved. It is difficult to describe this subject exhaustively because there are so many tendencies which have to be tested in combination that it is not possible to enumerate all of them.

In friendship there must also be no compulsion. An action may never be undertaken against better judgement because a friend so wishes it. Only after joint scrutiny should a decision be reached.

Friendship in the true sense of the word can only exist between good people. The prerequisite, therefore, is great spiritual maturity and a soul development that promises pure harmony. Therefore, between friends there can never arise a doubt as to whether a contemplated action is good or bad, because less mature souls are not sufficiently developed for friendship.

The notion of friendship, according to individual psychology, hardly measures up to the way I have described it. And it could hardly be applied to a person who is asked about it in earthly existence.

True friendship is also not something open to great discussion. It lies deep within a person and is taboo the material surroundings.

Let us therefore rather substitute the word "companionship" for friendship, and investigate whether a person is forced, either due to his surroundings or the tasks that he has to fulfil, to be alone and cut off from human society, or whether he goes to the other extreme and his entire abilities are concentrated only on giving pleasure to so-called friends and allowing them to participate in his wealth or superior knowledge etc. This is just as wrong as total seclusion.

I have already stated that good deeds are only those which benefit the community, and as such they are the only ones which assist one's progress.

The community is everything in life. It is much more so when earthly life ends. We fully understand it only on arriving here and after having realised where the infinite laws guide us and which goals are envisaged for us in the great, divine realm.

One fine day, in many million years, all individual spirit entities will become a single, shining power. It cannot be described in earthly words, so I will not speak more about this. There is only one thing you should know: all who are wandering around the universe singly, alone and often in an apparently abandoned fashion, as people imagine it, will flow into a commmunity of equal power, beauty, and wisdom.

In this sense friendship on earth is a small, modest beginning. Enough for today.

Ways of studying the ideal human.

TODAY we start a new chapter although there is still much to be said about friendship. This will follow later.

I want to discuss the way in which science must probe the true correlations in the life of man; how through correct observation a reasonably suitable assessment can be gained.

We have already seen that in this life nobody can personify an ideal human because the present stage of development of humanity is inadequate. It will be a long time before ideal humans are found in the material sphere of the world. According to man's own opinion, yes, perhaps, but as he lacks spiritual insight, his concept must needs be limited. The purpose of this work is to help mankind in some small way to realise that it must aspire to a much higher goal than the one which presently seems desirable.

It is known that great success can only be achieved if a person's sights are set high and the goal is pursued with all the power of one's spirit and soul. Once the desired objective has been achieved, we know from experience that it often seems small and futile, that one has overestimated its value or that it was not at all worth going after.

More often than not this applies to the accumulation of riches and wealth. If a rich person does not appraise and use his wealth correctly, this means in accordance with the infinite laws of nature, he will never be happier than somebody who lives in modest circumstances. It is a responsibility, often a great commitment and sometimes a very severe test, no less than the test of hardship and misery for another person.

The concepts here and on earth are so different that one could say that what I write is nonsense because only a materially secure existence can offer happiness. I have already said that only a few people will be able to follow what I say and understand it correctly.

On the material plane people do not yet have the ability to grasp matters which we impart from our more advanced standpoint. This is why it is already a great step forward when people make the effort to find the happy medium in all matters. But the recognition that it exists and the ability to find it presupposes that one is aware of the two extremes – spiritually seen, of course – for only then can one speak of a happy medium. The higher the upper end is placed, the higher will be the happy medium that one aspires to follow.

It is always only matter which prevents people adopting the middle course whichever sphere of earthly existence we consider.

Therefore science would first have to establish the happy medium and pave the way for the education of humanity according to this example.

However it should not be assumed that in all spheres of worldly life every human may become the embodiment of an ideal. As I have already explained, this depends on the task that the spirit entity has set himself for his earthly existence. Then again the ideal may be according to earthly man's viewpoint, but it is not the one I have mentioned as being the highest goal.

No earthly person is in a position to imagine or describe such an ideal, because to do so he would have to be at such a stage of evolution where he would no longer have to undergo the trials of earthly life. In every area of human life it is possible to research and identify what attitude, what deeds, foster the progress of mankind. One must only consider them from the viewpoint of the community and make all-encompassing love, wisdom and eternal order the basis. Whoever endeavours to research in this way cannot go wrong.

The second step now is to detect whether and how mankind, both collectively and individually, violates established norms. It is a mammoth task which only very few people can do. But these individuals will be found to lay the foundation for a healthy, moderate and natural attitude to life.

There is much that has to be pulled back from the extreme to a tolerable measure. Quite a few things need to be put into their true light. Others must receive more prominence than before.

For the time being I only give a general view of matters. Later I will go into more detail and suggest ways to create a basis for a healthy life and progress which is really desirable. One must only have the courage to begin.

Science will soon realise that in order to do this work it is necessary to divide it into many sections. It is not even possible to give a comprehensive picture in a short study. The main spheres of life have to be examined closely.

Whoever thinks he has only to check how the majority of people behave in various situations in life will soon be on the wrong track. Certain pointers can be taken from this, but very often one establishes that not only individuals, but all mankind is still erring and wandering along wrong paths.

I take just one example: technology. Man tends to equate the progress of technology with that of mankind. This is a great mistake. Technology has only been given to mankind so that life can be more pleasant, easier, healthier and natural. Where is this the case? Unfortunately all technology is exaggerated.

The knowledge of the infinite laws of nature, which a few initiates and scholars have made available to mankind, have been abused by crass materialists who think that everything is given only for the attainment of huge fortunes, riches, and material independence.

Independence is, on the whole, a miserable achievement, although I do not deny that material existence today is responsible for such a point of view. People must learn to achieve inner independence, the freedom of will, which naturally is subject to certain restrictions in material existence. But these must not cause people to have feelings of subservience.

Adaption through free will must be the basis for the progress of mankind; not orders on pain of penalties. How far removed mankind still is from such a point of view! At every corner there is a notice saying, "Forbidden to . . . " How seldom one reads, "The public, the residents, or the visitors are requested to . . . " Such a phrase appeals to personal free will more than all prohibitions or threats. People must realise this too. Somewhere in a city there must be a man who would take down all these – I would say brutal – signs and replace them with courteous requests. The results would be amazing. And the educational effect would not be long to follow.

It would be an example for business, professional and family behaviour and behaviour in all human relations. Try it, as it can do no harm! For example, if, instead of putting up a sign saying "No Trespassing" one put up one saying "Only staff may enter" many a person would read it with pleasure and understand it just as well as a strongly worded prohibition.

Here we have the second component of the basic conditions for the study of the human ideal.

It is free will, or better said, the freedom of the will. But the ideal human is not he who is aware of his free will and acts accordingly, but he who respects the free will of the next man and allows it free reign; he who does not force his own will on another person ruthlessly and egotistically. This brings us back to understanding and forgiving, which we have already discussed. There is scarcely a sphere in human existence where understanding and forgiving would not be required. Forgiving does not always infer indulgence for major mistakes and imperfections. It all depends on the case in point.

We spoke of the demands of civilisation. I would like to point out that the most important aspect of every investigation must be to study as to in how far this civilisation serves mankind and meets peoples' requirements for a materially and spiritually sound life. This civilisation is the basis of the community, of social life and its stability. As the body is the home of the individual spirit entity, so the achievements of civilisation are the basis of society. Society is a truly divine concept. Nothing can exist on its own in the universe; everything needs to be complemented, it requires help and support in order to develop. Whoever shuts himself off from the rest of the world will probably not perish. At the most he will vegetate in the material sense. What actually happens, as we see it from a more advanced point of view, is that he delays his progress.

The suffering and difficulties in the material world are, however, very unimportant in relation to the delay of spiritual progress. One only has to reflect what a short spell life on earth is compared with that in the spiritual sphere.

To live in the dark here is much harder than anyone can imagine. Trial and purification continue until the realisation dawns that egotism and contempt for society are mistakes, which must be resisted by every possible means.

On this note we shall stop. Next time we will write about the healthy conditions of life in a community, which is the prerequisite for successful, progressive existence.

The community and the necessary and proper attitude to be accorded to it.

THE theme for discussion today is the community.

Proceeding from the principle that nobody succeeds in achieving perfection and real success on his own, let us examine the aspects according to which a person has to choose the community to which he will belong and to which he decides to devote his services.

The wish to do so must be there in the first place. The community is not to be confused with the society into which the spirit entity has incarnated and is materially committed through birth.

In the first instance, the community is absolutely dependent on his philosophy of life and necessitates the right interpretation of it. It is not the environment in which the person lives which characterises society, but his interpretation of the purpose of life and the wish, which lies deep within, to fulfil his obligations to the community in accordance with his agreement expressed in the world beyond. Of course, I speak of those spirit entities who are role models for less mature characters and can be considered ideal.

At the outset people do not know what their task is, and only a few sense it early on. Through proper guidance, in good time in the formative years, a lot of help can be given and many a mistake avoided. It is therefore necessary to decide which career one is going to choose or which calling one will follow to be of service to mankind.

If there is no profession available to achieve the end in view as far as can be established, one can safely choose a banal career to keep oneself going until the right tasks – which need have nothing to do with one's career – are brought to one's notice.

For everybody has his good and often great guide whom he has only to obey. "Obey" not in the sense of total subservience, but in the sense of willingly listening to the inner voice, and willingly following his advice.

This must be stressed, to avoid the impression that a person finds the right way without effort on his part. On the contrary; only he can decide how he wishes to mould and organise his life. The opportunity to do so is given freely to him. He must only know how to take advantage of it.

Many a person goes into the world beyond and establishes that the tasks he had undertaken have not been fulfilled as would have been desirable and necessary for his progress. He has to make good.

I have already stated that this is exactly what happened to me because I did not have the courage to act and oppose all prejudices. Only a few succeed in completely fulfilling their tasks. Material life and its attendant material interpretation of the meaning of life is the blockage that is laid across our path, in accordance with the eternal, irrevocable laws of nature. It is the battle against this erroneous philosophy in earthly existence which rewards us with the maturity that will eventually free us from the bonds of materialism.

How are we to succeed? By having the correct attitude to the community in the knowledge that everybody is aiming for the same goal and has to do so, and in the conviction that for us too there is no decisive progress as long as souls in need of help still live in the dark.

We have only perfected our tasks when we have helped everybody to find the light. But how can the individual succeed in doing this? Never, you will say, and you are right. One does not fulfil one's duty by giving a poor person money, food, and a roof over his head. He has to be guided to accept the community so that one can expect him to show himself worthy of it through the same willingness to help others. The reception of comforts does not make for happiness and contentment. "To give is better than to receive" is an old proverb. It must only be properly understood.

Giving should not be confined to material goods. They are the very least. One sees this most noticeably where benefits bestowed on underdeveloped nations are simply wasted. They have not earned them, and were not in a position to earn them. Give them the opportunity to work for them and then you will receive real gratitude! Such help in the spiritual sense is a seed that assures a thousandful harvest.

It is not a matter of goods that are used up or consumed – and thereby lost. They only stimulate the desire for more and do not permit judgement as to their value and the amount of love and sense of duty required to make them available.

To lead, instruct and give spiritual guidance is the duty of people who work within the community and wish to live for it. Not with orders and prohibition, but with all-embracing love, with understanding and forgiveness, even at the risk that failure in the material sense is the result.

At the moment the earthly sphere is in an alarming state of turmoil and unrest. Great, radical changes or cataclysms will lead only gradually to purification. They are the result of incorrect social aid which has not – or only very seldom – resulted from an ideal attitude, but in the main is the work of greedy so-called capable business people. This cannot have good results. One cannot transform totally immature nations, who in addition live in quite exceptional climatic conditions, into civilised communities from one day to the next. They will always consider these efforts as totally foreign and disturbing and continue to fall back on their own instincts and particularities until, after many generations, an acceptable standard is achieved.

The highest principle is that there may not be any coercion in material and spiritual life. One has only to look at the black population of the United States. They were imported as slaves, underdeveloped masses, and put to heavy work like animals. But their spiritual development did not proceed any faster, simply because they had to labour in a foreign corner of the earth. They needed just as long as they would have done on their home ground. But they were constantly confronted with the prosperity of the West and the generations born there in the meantime now claim equal rights and non-discrimination as resident citizens, according to the laws of nature, and equal rights.

All the great conflicts in progress are the results of mistakes committed a long time ago. But the time will come when this will be quite clearly realised and only then shall the possibility be given to introduce peace and quiet in the material world.

Recognition of the basic mistakes and shortcomings are the first requirements to be fulfilled. Above all, over and over again it is the incorrect interpretation of the community and the service to be accorded to it. This service may not be turned into a business or gone about in a way that implies material benefit. Some good beginnings have been made but they are a drop in the bucket.

The Church has concerned itself very much with the education of people in the Christian faith in the well-meant opinion that its faith alone is the only true one. This was a big mistake and has had to prove a failure in the same way as, in civilised countries, it has gradually to work towards a change if it does not wish to be completely spurned by humanity.

The Church is a very useful institution ordained by God. But it has failed to realise its task and has not found the right way to enable it to become a God-given tool. Everything needs time. Gradually, also here, knowledge shall dawn and the task to serve the community in the divine sense will be heard in the correct harmony; by this I mean it will be correctly discerned and interpreted by those entrusted and called to the work.

When I spoke of harmony, it was because divine tasks and service in the truly divine sense are clothed in musical tones that are barely to be understood and described in the earthly sense. Good church music is a pale but faithful reflection, a modest beginning of the great and unbelievably beautiful music of the spheres. This explains my slip of tongue in the previous paragraph.

So, to cultivate, to serve the community does not only mean to provide a basis for existence in the material sense, but above all it means to help people to proceed on their own on the way to progress. This is done much less through good lessons and enforced confessions than through an exemplary life.

Only free will should induce imitation. Progress can never be forced. If it is, it is not genuine progress, even though it may appear to be so in the material sense.

How many scholars have made discoveries without the intention of using them for war and destruction. But incorrectly educated people have been led to the use of these achievements without having been called to do so, and misused them for harnessing the forces of Nature as ordained by God.

Too little attention is paid to free will. People are still too influenced by the desire for power and the craving for personal prestige and are therefore of the opinion that they have to impose their own point of view, their own will, on the souls who have been entrusted – or are subservient – to them. They often do this with the best of intentions, for lack of better knowledge.

One can only serve the community if one follows these basic rules in all matters and always pays attention to them. Exemplify what serves and advances the community, introduce and aspire to be an example of spiritual maturity and a healthy philosophy of life and you will see the result, not on the masses, but on the individual in his daily life.

To set an example educates and education is an aid and a service to the community. Everybody can offer this service without a particular calling and he will earn one as a result. It is a possibility offered to all humanity; it leads to self education and through this to a healthy and happy community to live in.

Next time I will talk about the relationship between a calling and the community.

The divine sense of a calling.

I HAVE already clarified the distinction between a career and a calling and will now try and characterise the meaning of a calling.

A calling is an assignment bestowed from spiritual heights which even we here are not able to see. The prerequisite is particular gifts in a certain field, but only those abilities which serve all mankind. On no account do these include those that fuel greed or lust for power, or ones which have a purely physical origin and are steeped in pleasure in the material sense. These abilities are worthless as they cannot lead to spiritual progress – either for those who practise them or those who enjoy them.

A calling does not require a considerably highly developed maturity. It may be bestowed on beginners who develop slowly in repeated incarnations to a level above the general stream. In the first instance I will deal with the calling to be a doctor and helper of mankind and in this context proceed from my own experiences, which in earthly life I did not realise, at least not consciously. But today from my more elevated and freer viewpoint I can contemplate them far better and more correctly. I would like to disclose – if I may use this phrase – things which will be able to contribute to a positive way of thinking for a career and a calling.

Many hundred years ago I freely chose the career of doctor and soon realised it was one of the most important for suffering mankind. As an alchemist I carried out research because I was conscious of the fact that around us forces were at work which we were not familiar with, but which, according to divine decree, we should nevertheless avail ourselves of. Today there are no longer alchemists; only the technique prevails which, without being bound to the eternal laws or Nature, quite logically continues to build onto the rudiments which the inspired initiates bequeathed to posterity. There are still such initiates today, but contact with extra-terrestrial powers has faded into the background.

Conceit and selfishness, ambition and the striving for power prevent people from acknowledging influences other than those which are materially understandable. These are intelligence and knowledge. This is extreme egotism, for in point of fact, all great discoveries come from the extra-terrestrial sphere. Nobody is in a position to discover something new without his good, selfless guides who make suggestions to him and point the way. Not quite without personal merit of course; there must always be a good, strong will in a position to grasp an opportunity.

Inventors have seldom achieved material recognition and riches. They were well aware that it was not their achievement alone, and their advanced philosophy of life did not allow them to make a business of it. People feel sorry for such poor souls who have often died in impoverished circumstances. It is not so. Progress is made at a higher level. This my earlier explanations made clear.

Quite apart from this, people are often not in agreement with the teachings and explanations of such initiates and wise persons dedicated to their calling. They oppose them because they do not conform to their dearly beloved material philosophy of life. They only want to enjoy themselves and think that to do so no higher spiritual values are necessary. Afterwards, the realisation is bitter and not only personal progress but that of humanity generally is retarded.

To repeat what I have already explained: only the community can cause the spirit to progress – a community that is healthy not only from the material, but also from the emotional and spiritual point of view. This is why, again and again, advanced souls are called to work towards this goal selflessly and without material encumbrances.

A divinely inspired person who is so far beyond materialism that he can live and work without it is a Messiah. He has achieved spiritual maturity and purity of soul through the activation of free will and personifies an ideal and a helper in the purest sense of a "calling." Jesus Christ was such a Messiah. He was – and is – not the first and certainly not the last to be sent to help people attain their goal, a goal that everybody must attain one day.

Judging from the misinterpretations attributed to his teachings, we can unfortunately see how far humanity is from the goal that it must attain. Nevertheless, the appearance of a great initiate in the material world always indicates progress, if not for all people then at least for a considerable number of them.

The resistance to new teachings which such spirit entities bring to the world of materialism stimulates people. They inspire them to investigate, and to think. After a period of many errors and wrong conclusions true knowledge must dawn one day.

Humanity is still like a small child. The experiences and knowledge of earlier existences slumber within it, but only after a hard battle can it achieve realisation and further progress. But it would be desirable that those called to spread good teachings – the priests – would finally realise that they are building on sand if they make hard and fast rules of communications of olden days instead of searching for the truth themselves. For this is the great mistake the Church makes. It is not good and it is not right that it feels itself bound to dogmas and doctrines and does not believe it is allowed to deviate from them. Instead, it should treat them as foundations to build upon.

It is the fear of censure by the masses which – without giving the matter much thought – causes it to cling to long-standing doctrines and customs instead of taking the development of humanity into account and proceeding from the assumption that everything is in a constant state of flux and requires constant renewal. It appears that in Church circles the knowledge of this great truth is maturing. With continued spiritual development and increasing maturation the wish for reform and stimulation is dawning. It is time that the high dignitaries of the Church face this fact and make the effort to introduce radical changes, otherwise it will be too late and time will be lost. It may be very long before a new Messiah is able to bring truth and good teachings to the material world.

But primarily I want to write about the calling of a doctor. To do this we must proceed once again from the assumption – and remind ourselves – that every illness is located in the soul. And in addition to physical treatment, a doctor's duty is to care for the soul and heal it.

We have heard that the soul clothes the spirit and is the link that binds it to the body; that it is an extremely fine and sensitive instrument and requires delicate, careful handling. To offer such treatment, the doctor must have achieved a high degree of knowledge and emotional maturity. Knowledge gleaned from books is not sufficient for medicine today. The main basis is a mature, superior personality.

Bear in mind that the patient has – and should have – the greatest confidence in his doctor. He would not even be as candid with his priest as he is with his doctor.

Everybody can glean knowledge from books if he studies long enough and is willing to learn. A mature soul needs more than this.

This is why we have to differentiate between so-called doctors who study and practise medicine as a trade; who treat a patient as a case and not as a highly individual personality requiring total sympathetic understanding and care in his treatment, and practitioners who are the true servants of mankind; who are aware of their higher calling and are grateful to serve. Here too differences in personal maturity are not to be avoided because doctors are also evolving and are certainly not perfect and inviolable. But their aspiration is to be dependable in their conduct and their profession.

Those with a calling have a hard life, according to materially minded people, because only their work gives them pleasure and satisfaction. Materially minded individuals have no way of knowing what satisfaction such a philosophy of life can give. Of course, this does not only apply to doctors even it they have the greatest possibilities of helping mankind to progress.

People do not only need a healthy body and soul in order to progress. Care of the soul can only be effectively achieved with positive measures.

I have already mentioned that music plays a great role as the main element of extra-terrestrial powers of nature. In this sphere too there are great people who have been called. They are not always amongst people on earth. It would be too much of a good thing and taken for granted if pleasure were so richly given.

In the same way that great initiates and Messiahs are not always on earth but are sent when Divine Discretion judges the time to be right, so too great musicians are only granted to earth infrequently and at great intervals.

Just as Messiahs are in touch with great leaders in the world beyond and consciously make use of their help, so too great composers are in touch with extra-terrestrial powers of the universe and receive from high spheres the music which they pass on to mankind. As I have already mentioned, this is not to be interpreted in relation to space. They are the appropriate recipients for rays from very elevated spirit heights. It is the power of the rays sent to them that enables the wonderful works to be created. They are mediums in the true sense of the word and, depending on the stage of development of their souls, recipients of the most beautiful tones from the spheres.

People who react very strongly when they listen to good music can gradually achieve advanced spiritual maturity, so that they become recipients and creators of music that has eternal power.

The cultivation of music and the learning of an instrument induces a state of receptivity in the soul; this may give rise to vital energy or heal a sick soul.

Enough for today. Next time we will speak of other forms of art and those called to them.

Art, its origin and its evaluation.

WHAT actually is art? According to the type of art, it is the highest degree of proficiency and talent, of inspiration and individualism that man can achieve. In music individualism is not always an advantage. Inspiration is the focal issue. Music is basic art. The musician cannot gradually attain heights of achievement by learning as one learns a trade, but from the outset he enjoys a certain degree of inspiration and must perfect it with well-learned technique.

It is a different matter where artists who are craftsmen are concerned. For them technique and skill are of prime importance and they have to combine these with ideas which, in the main, also come from other spheres. For craftsmen too help may come from without if these powers are granted entry and peace. Introspectiveness in the true sense of the word provides the basic elements.

Introspectiveness means to perceive in the innermost depths the work to be created while eliminating all influences from the material sphere, thereby achieving concentration in great peace without strain and with totally positive thought. Introspectiveness is given when people are concerned with spiritual matters because this can only be achieved in isolation from material influences.

It is only in a state of introspection that artistic work in the true sense of the word can be developed and brought to perfection; a perfection as it is understood by mankind.

What today is described as art is often miserable handicraft, or not even that, because handicraft presupposes that something is completed with a degree of perfection.

Painting should only be considered to have artistic value if it portrays perfection in a certain direction. There are very good guidelines that enable the value of a painting to be established. The opinion of friends or laymen is not authoritative. Only great artists can pass proper judgement on art.

But art can also develop from sheer skill. It is a work practised by man through free will with stamina and patience and developed to a supreme achievement which is the exception rather than the rule.

Art is not art simply because the next person cannot paint or draw; it must rank above the run of the mill level and have such a powerful effect that it serves to point man in certain directions or encourages him to develop his spiritual knowledge.

Edification and spiritual development flow from the art of song combined with music, and from the spoken word combined with poetry.

The poet who is able to create abiding art is, in most cases, mediumistically inclined. He brings the predisposition for his activity in this sphere with him from an earlier life and receives help and support from the world beyond. According to his willingness and spiritual level, the rays that influence and help him come from the corresponding level in the world beyond.

The more man is in a position to open himself to the powers from the universe and is willing to do so, the more advanced the spirits are who adopt him and his art. This art shall not only serve as edification, but also as instruction and point humanity to progress. The theatre is not only a place of edification but should – and this people have realised already to a great extent – have an educational effect; it should always refer to the infinite, irrefutable laws of nature. The actors have to convey these valuable educational topics.

The presentation of characters which they portray must be so impressive, so true to life, that people are inspired to think about them and forced to decide which character studies it would be desirable to reject or emulate. It is a great, magnificent task if the subject presented is also noble and valuable.

Times change, and so do people. Taste in every form of art is changing. Any judgement as to what is good and valuable must nevertheless be formed from a more advanced viewpoint; a work of art should not be considered as such simply because it appeals to a larger crowd of people and gives more pleasure than one which is only recognised and treasured by a few.

Art is simply a creation of inspired people, of which there are only a few on earth. No work of art requires an endless or even a very long time to complete. Everything promoted from the world beyond is brought forth without consideration of the time factor.

One has only to think in how short a time great composers have written their symphonies and concertos; in how short a time great philosophers and poets have completed a whole series of books that contain momentous knowledge.

Everything realised by inspiration is more or less free from material inhibitions. More or less, because it depends on the medium's willingness to be receptive. An actor is different. He has to rely on an excellent memory, but inspiration could also give him all the necessary guidance that would enable him to present a correct and powerful interpretation of the character he portrays. If an actor is really blessed, he must approach his studies introspectively. Talent and the ability to communicate are the natural prerequisites for success in this field.

By talent I mean the ability to perform exactly in accordance with the role and to have an excellent vocal command as far as delivery and resonance are concerned. Not many have this gift so one can safely say that only a few have talent. A melodious voice and a clear delivery are a pleasure for the audience and command attention. The art lies in adapting the character's speech and presentation in a suitable manner

Only perseverance and constant practice lead to a true and enduring result.

Natural talent and acquired knowledge. How to recognise and cultivate them. The conviction of progress in the right direction.

TODAY I want to describe the correlations between natural talent and knowledge acquired through diligence and hard work.

There is a big difference between these two components. If they are combined, people on earth believe that a perfection exceeding normal measure can be achieved. But seen from here, from the world beyond, this combination is quite normal and the most desirable and obvious course of development. On earth the existing circumstances and the general or predominant stages of development cause this to be regarded as something unusual.

There are careers and callings which require a basis in the spiritual sphere as well as refinement of technique in the material sphere.

Pure music in its perfect state only exists in the spiritual sphere. But for people to enjoy it, instruments, notes and interpreters are necessary. It is easy to imagine the countless errors and shortcomings that occur if so many material aids are necessary to produce music on earth.

This is why there is no music of the spheres in its pure form in the world. The great masters of this art form have, through perseverance and diligence and, of course, with an equal amount of dedication, brought all their powers to bear and attracted all available help from the extra-terrestrial sphere in order to make available to mankind what they experienced and heard in its purest form in their innermost souls.

The correlation between outside energies and the input of the composer result in an achievement which is beyond human understanding.

This is why nobody can simply say, "I want to be a composer" if he has no indication of talent. In spite of great zeal and dedication he will achieve nothing, or very little. He is able to produce tone pictures in the style of the great masters, but they will scarcely have permanent value and make little impression on the human soul.

But should a person have, or feel the sounds of eternal music within, he has only to seek meditation, avoid disturbances and allow the divine strains to take effect in peace and total introspection.

Many a person has heard these tones and been totally absorbed by them, but neglected to acquire the necessary technical skills in order to interpret them and so has not made use of his gift for humanity. This is a sin of omission, for everybody is obliged to serve the community with every fibre of his being and achieve results. Not to do so is to disregard the bestowal of a divine favour and obstructs progress for a long time.

Technical skill is something everybody can learn. There are many so-called artists who are able to interpret the work of great masters in a brilliant fashion. They are already laying the foundations in earthly life for a calling at a later stage – the basis for the bestowal of ultimate grace for human beings. They are destined to create the most beautiful earthly music in the cosmos,

Just as in music there is a divine calling and material technical training which can rise to great heights due to free will, so it is in all branches of the most beautiful arts. The painter too is led and receives help from the world beyond. He sees – I would say – in the way the composer hears.

Seeing in the earthly world and in the world beyond are quite different. A mature soul can see into profound depths, can have a spiritual – or better said – an emotional understanding which is not possible in a purely material sense. It is actually not to be compared with the normal act of seeing.

The really inspired artist experiences the pictures he paints and, like a writing medium, his hand must obey the command of his experience and conjure the deeply sensed picture onto the canvas. This, anyway, is how the layman sees it. This art is also divinely inspired and must be cultivated by thorough technical training.

In this sphere too there have been many lost opportunities due to faulty education and the restrictions which material life produces. Many a talent from a previous life or from the world beyond and much help offered by extra-terrestrial spirits is either not recognised or simply rejected; natural talents are allowed to atrophy simply because materialism has a stronger hold than divinely inspired mental activity.

Notwithstanding, a ray of hope is apparent on earth. More and more, people realise that the cultivation of the arts and sciences, regardless of their material outcome, have a higher value in human existence than was thought up till now.

So much for the correlations and complements between the spiritual and the earthly in art. I have dwelt on art to begin with because both components can more readily be understood in this form. In point of fact, such a complement and correlation exists in all professions and occupations that serve the human community. How, we will examine more closely.

A teacher, for example, is a leader and educator and is greatly responsible for talents going to waste and abilities being hampered when they could have reached a high stage of development.

A teacher must be more than just an imparter of knowledge of essential and interesting matters. He must either have, or strive to obtain, the ability to study the souls of the young people entrusted to him and highlight and encourage their more or less evident abilities. If he is not able to do this, he has to ensure that the youngsters pass into the right hands and are helped to cultivate their natural talents.

How often does a teacher realise that his student soon ranks above him and has surpassed him in art or science, for this is how it must be.

The generation of today is blazing a trail for the generation of tomorrow which with its knowledge and abilities, and in its spiritual development must outgrow the former, otherwise there is no progress.

This is why people should remember that they are not necessarily more mature on account of greater age. They should acknowledge that they have a lot to learn from the younger generation and accept it. How often people express surprise that small children today are much more mature and spiritually more developed than they were at that age. Of course, this has a lot to do with material development in the technical field and so on, because the living conditions are generally better now than when we were young.

But apart from this, many spirit entities who return to the material world are more advanced and indeed very noticeably so. This is due to their efforts in the world beyond and the knowledge acquired from their spiritual schooling.

This is a big comfort in a world so shaken by disturbances. I must therefore always repeat that only progress is to be achieved, even though the material world seems doomed. And because it seems so, it is so important to be convinced of positive progress and essential to bear in mind the limited worth of matter.

Next time I will write about a sound interpretation of earthly life and try to give some guidelines as to how to find and maintain the happy medium when eventually the realisation dawns that this is the only correct attitude.

Knowledge about the correlations with the world beyond as a basis for a sound philosophy of life and education.

TODAY I want to speak about how important it is for people continually to bear in mind the correlations with the world beyond so that it is possible for them to develop a sound and correct philosophy of life.

Once again I would like to repeat that firstly, everybody comes to earth with a complete blueprint and that everyone has a unique personality which cannot be identical with any other.

Secondly, it must be stressed that nobody is forced to achieve anything; certainly not by Fate, as one tends to say, or by foreign spirit entities – unless he is possessed.

At this stage we want to discuss people who have already found the way to progress and, in the interest of further quest and development along this way, have taken it upon themselves to accept the tests of the material world. They must be the first to be reviewed because they should be the teachers and leaders and shining examples to other, weaker and less developed fellow beings.

But in so doing, we must above all bear in mind that a person who has passed from extra-terrestrial existence to earthly life neither knows nor is aware of the capabilities he has brought with him from the world beyond. If, on entering the material world, we knew which assignments and trials we had volunteered to take upon ourselves, it would in many respects be easier but often catastrophic as well. For instance, a spirit entity can be born into an environment that is so difficult that his soul can hardly develop as it had intended. Ill-health caused by the environment can also be a significant handicap which sometimes is not absolutely desirable and is not taken into consideration by Omnipotence.

By this I mean to say that not everything is pre-planned in every detail; only the broad outlines are there. After this it depends what help and how much energy a spirit entity has available to face all obstacles and difficulties and overcome them in such a way that the plan brought along becomes quite clear and the person is able to head straight for his goal. It is easy to imagine how numerous the obstacles can be along life's way and how they impede him.

The most important component for the achievement of life's goal is free will. In the long run no obstacle will be able to delay progress. The plan for life matures and becomes obvious sooner or later. There is no need to be afraid of making a mistake if one follows the right path towards lucidity.

Now let us examine this path. In the first years of life the care of the body and soul is entrusted to parents and teachers. They must be aware of the enormity of the task which has been assigned to them and which they have accepted in good faith, with a pure heart and with great love. They lay the most important foundations for the development of the spirit and soul of the child.

The biggest mistake that is so often made in this regard is the incorrect interpretation of the meaning of education. A child always endeavours to imitate adults, to copy their habits and learn to speak the way they do. Adults just cannot imagine how receptive a child is. According to the maturity of the spirit entity within, every impression creates a very exact concept. In the good sense this is very valuable, but in a bad environment or in a case of thoughtless reaction it can be dangerous. Dangerous, that is, in so far as the progress of the child's development is concerned. This is why children ought not to grow up in the company of a great many people, but should be given the opportunity to become aware gradually of their powers or energies within the family circle.

In quiet play a child often expresses the basic aspects of the blueprint it has brought to earth. If this is constantly disturbed, perhaps by unreasonable requests of civilisation and society, the nervous system can unintentionally be overstimulated, which leads to the conclusion that the child is wayward and naughty.

I have already mentioned that the child is best educated by example and the parents have the duty of offering it mental stimulation. By this I mean that already as an infant the child must be given the opportunity to exercise its own will. In this way it will become aware of its energies and be able to take on all tasks which it has voluntarily set for itself.

Children who are described as good, who never go against the will of their parents are, in the main, weak-willed and in later life more prone to defeat by difficulties. People who as children were self-willed cope with such difficulties very easily.

If parents have the correct concept and understanding of the purpose of life and are fully aware of their great task then, through constant observation of their child, they will soon be aware of its abilities and seek to develop them.

So the beginning of the life path is not left to the discretion of the child but predominantly to its parents and the people around it. Only with increasing maturity, not maturity of the spirit entity which lies dormant within the person at a very specific stage of development, but maturity of thought which is linked to the development of the mind, does the power of discrimination gradually grow; not according only to feeling as is the case in early childhood, but with intelligence and good sense which only in the course of time is activated to its potential.

It is to be understood that intelligence, knowledge and, perhaps too, wisdom are all incarnated with the spirit entity. But only after development and the healthy growth of the organs – in this case particularly, the mind – can they be expressed and recognised by those around him.

Quite early in life man makes his own decisions. His will soon guides him how to follow the path and which goal he wishes to attain. Both teachers and parents must constantly bear this in mind. It is quite in order for them to try and direct the child's free will onto the right track. Direct does not mean force. Good experiences from one's own life can give a direction, but may not be forced upon anybody as proven prerequisites for the next generation.

It has so often been the case that the experiences of the older generation are no longer valid for the next one in a steadily changing world. When man reaches the stage that he begins to wonder what purpose his existence could possibly have; when he starts to search out the tasks which he will set for himself in order to achieve that material and spiritual satisfaction, both for his personal ego and for the community, then it is time to tell him, in plain language, the fundamental truths about human life, Omnipotence and the eternal laws of nature, thereby steering the teaching onto the right path.

Everybody who is already at a higher stage of development will be happy to accept this and strive to make use of the good cosmic influences. The peace and security that he attains in this way will accelerate him along his life's path and make him, in turn, a guide –

and an example for others.

If a person wishes to enhance his spirituality, he must above all not be caught up in material concerns and conditions, not become dependent on them, which means not to regard riches as the most desirable gift from Heaven.

All knowledge and all ability must be directed to the benefit of the community or, at least, society. I have already touched on the difference between the community and society, but I would like to reiterate what I have said.

Society is, as it were, the result of civilisation. Its level is commensurate with its prevailing stage of development, the union of people mainly of the same type and with common interests. In the harmony of their souls and the congruity of their spiritual endeavours they must both complement and assist one another, whether it be in the edifying and scientific fields or in the purely material one, such as handicraft work. For both groups, community and society, the common link is mutual agreement and co-operation.

Serving the community, however, means to help those who are less developed; it means to serve the poor and those in need of support; to show them the path of progress and to direct and guide them

The community is not characterised by levels of society. It is everywhere because the concept of high and low is not identical with a highly and less developed spirit entity.

I have already mentioned that people will have to discriminate according to these principles; that it is not the material frame but the value of the painting – as I would say – which is the criterion. Then we will only refer to the community and not have to differentiate between social levels and the community. In the latter, all are equal, it is only the tasks that are different. That is all for today, but I will speak again about the path to a sound philosophy of life.

The path to a sound philosophy of life.
The appraisal of matter.

THIS subject is very extensive and many roads lead to the optimal state of mind. By this I mean to say that everybody has his own idea of how to attain it. As no two people are alike, the procedure, thinking and feeling must be individual.

But notwithstanding, there must be principles that are alike. Those should be observed by everybody who wants to achieve what he has in mind. The only difference lies in how to do it and the divergence of spiritual maturity.

Let us study the various possibilities – the common criteria – without judgement as to how such principles should be observed.

For this we must imagine a person who has to follow his path quite independently; we will not consider that in his childhood there may have been obstacles and hindrances to overcome and assume that this person possesses a spiritual maturity that qualifies him for independent thought. The path is quite clearly defined. It leads straight to the goal. He does not have to look left or right.

Childhood is the age of opinions that are totally unaffected; of spontaneous views free of mistrust. Every impression is absorbed by the spirit and soul, both still unclouded by experiences which only in later life can dim the clear view and influence personal judgement.

The child lets a picture, an animal, a person, affect it. By this I mean to say that without reflection it feels the radiation only with the power of its soul and thereby the value of whoever or whatever it comes up against. This is why children are much more honest than adults in their likes and dislikes as long as their feelings are not under control and constraint.

If a person is able to maintain the freedom of his soul and allows his feelings to react quite spontaneously in his perceptions and judgements, then his opinions about people and things around him will hardly ever be wrong. But this is an ideal state of affairs, which man can barely attain in his earthly existence. Matter, the environment, civilisation – all disturb his feelings and force him to stray far away from his own path.

But if a person could judge in a totally uninfluenced and unimpeded fashion, then an incorrect approach to life is out of the question. Only a positive lifeline would be found and followed because the basic fundamentals in everybody are good; only bad influences of the past or the present darken and bury them.

A person would not have to learn why he was living in this material world. His feelings, in this case his good contact to his spirit guide, would enable him to see the right path.

The correct philosophy of life, above all, embraces the knowledge for the reason of earthly existence; the conviction that it is only a preparation for a higher life, and that this necessitates the accomplishment of good deeds in the striving for spiritual maturity.

This attitude holds matter and earthly goods of little account, but this, however, does not mean that one is allowed to spurn and despise or even reject them totally.

As long as man is bound to matter he is dependent on it. But it is necessary to appraise and value this dependence correctly; one should not be overpowered and suffocated by it.

As has been expressed so often, matter should only serve, not dominate. The correct approach to life, therefore, includes the ability to find the right measure in the appraisal of matter; both over-rating and under-rating it are equally detrimental. For instance, people who despise matter and only devote themselves to their spiritual life often neglect the care of their bodies and their health because they resent wasting time on them, time away from their spiritual activities. They only think to make up for this attitude when they realise that their spirit cannot keep up with what they have undertaken without a healthy body. But how often is it too late, and severe disturbances of the nervous system put an early end to the well-meant endeavours.

It must be stressed again and again that the material world permits a sound approach to life to be formed if a person has a clear view of the path that has been mapped out for his eternal life. A clear view does not mean complete knowledge of the events in earthly existence. It means awareness of the general direction that is the same for all mankind: the striving for spiritual perfection and harmony with the infinite.

The tasks in material life are infinitesimal – and this must be known – because accord with infinity implies more than only being good in the earthly sense. Matter gives the opportunity to seek and find the right measure which leads to peace and harmony for spiritual progress.

In all matters and all life's situations there is a middle course. It is the path that leads straight to the goal and is the only one that allows man to be really happy.

So we already have some components that can lead to a sound and correct attitude to life. They are available to everybody: all should apply them. Whoever is blessed with too many material goods in life will soon discover that they are a burden, not a joy. Of course, one takes it for granted that in his striving for a correct attitude to life he sees things in their right prospective and is severely critical of himself. Generally this is a person who is willing to let others share his wealth and does not live in constant dread of starving to death if he gives away something. To dispose of everything is not right, nor does anybody expect him to do so. Moderation is his guideline.

It also does not depend on the verdict of fellow men who consider that a rich person must be evil rather than good. Not all wealthy people are rich because of greed and acquisitiveness, or envy and egotism. In this respect the degree of prosperity is like all the fundamentals of earthly existence.

They are determined according to infinite laws and bestowed on people with explicit directions and conditions as to the tests to be undergone in order to reach spiritual perfection.

One must constantly bear in mind that happiness or unhappiness on earth, according to the earthly concept of these conditions, is totally unimportant. What really fosters progress is to be judged and valued quite differently. But man only sees this when he has left the material world and looks back with spiritual eyes at earthly life which has ended.

This is why people should always be aware of the fact that all the worries and sorrows of earthly existence are so negligible compared with the monumental tasks that lie ahead and which, with goodwill and spiritual maturity, invariably contribute to their pleasure and real happiness. So I appeal to all aspiring persons of goodwill: do not succumb to the worries and difficulties of daily life and let them get you down. They are so trivial and irrelevant compared with the glorious ascent that awaits you in the world beyond.

With such a positive attitude, with the ability to deal with this appeal, it must be easy to find the correct point of view for every situation in life. Happiness and confidence must be the keynote of every undertaking, then there can be no failure. From the achievement comes renewed strength.

Suffering and pain must also be judged positively. They cannot be ignored. In earthly life they are the touchstones and give doubting and erring people the greatest maturity, the surest pointers.

Bodily suffering and pain are not necessary in the world beyond; there are other ways and aids here for dealing with errors and doubt. Of course I speak of those who have risen above the darkness and individuals whose spiritual maturity has permitted them to cast a glance upwards.

I have already mentioned that it is worthwhile to suffer the pains and sorrows of earthly existence. The reward for great patience is a wonderful existence in the world beyond.

There are still several comments I have to make and explain on this subject, but for today I will close. I hope that I have been a stimulus for reflection – in the good sense – and caused some people to check their own lives and their own opinions of material things.

The value of matter to be considered when searching for life's path.

TODAY I want to discuss how everybody can discover a philosophy of life which is the right one for him.

We have already heard that there is no hard and fast universal way of establishing this because everybody is unique: his opinion of life and its purpose must be in accordance with his spiritual maturity.

But it is important whether this expressed opinion stems from personal reflection or if the influence of family and friends has played a part in forming and moulding it. This is why repeatedly we find that people only attain their personal views on the world and life when they reach a ripe old age and have learned their lessons through personal experiences.

We must therefore presume that it is not easy for the individual to establish a mental attitude to life without resorting to or adopting the example of others.

And now, as always, it depends primarily on the stage of development of the spirit entity and the soul as to how far the person is dependent on others or can already at an early age create his own philosophy born of his free will.

Once again, it is the duty of parents and teachers to be good leaders and helpers. On the one hand they must leave the child or youngster to develop free will and thought; on the other, they ought to intervene should it establish an incorrect outlook. So in this era of materialism and excessive dependence on earthly goods we must consider that those who are mature, the adults, have to be pointed in the right direction to help them find a correct viewpoint on life and combat their mistakes. They in turn will then create the correct fundamental principles for the future generation who, following the good example created for them, will unfailingly find the right path.

Of course, this cannot be achieved overnight, which means in one generation. There are still many people who have not progressed. Great patience is required to inch forward little by little in order to bring about the desired result. I will now explain how this can be done.

The first lesson, I would say, is to make known the fundamental truths of eternal life, the invisible correlations with the world beyond and recurring incarnation.

The wish to aspire to this much higher life in the fourth dimension must be awakened in individuals so that they prepare themselves for it and carry out all tasks that are set for them with courage and patience – in short, that they seek to make progress. People must learn to recognise and understand the overall pattern of their life on earth and in the world beyond; they must be convinced that these correlations are good and correct. It is the duty of those who have been called to convince them. This is primarily the Church and psychotherapists or doctors in general if I may proceed on the assumption that medical science has adopted my views expressed in earlier chapters and works on the premise that every illness is based in the soul, and every psychic disease or handicap is caused by an incorrect approach to life.

As I have pointed out, one depends on the other. But for every treatment and every cure an examination of the patient's mental attitude to life is important. I have drawn attention to the basic elements, which are the same for everybody.

The second step is for the individual to establish which of the tasks set for him in earthly life can or should be fulfilled. Here, for the first time, the maturity of the spirit and the condition of the soul are to be taken into consideration because everybody must be able to understand the fundamental truths.

They must only be made known generally. In order to fulfil the tasks and tests one has taken on, without being able to determine too clearly what they are, one requires the ability to test oneself, to translate wishes into deeds. This has always to be done in the knowledge that the accomplishment of tasks in material life should never serve the purpose of accumulating goods, but ought to help to develop spirit and soul.

This will not be accomplished by equalising all peoples' material possessions. It is not left to earthly powers to determine where the boundaries lie in order to let apparent justice reign in this direction.

The eternal laws of nature seem to make provision for weaker and stronger, poorer and richer, healthier and sicker people. Everything either depends on or is justified by free will and the dissimilar development that stems from it.

The attitude to material goods and the significance attached to them in earthly life is a special chapter which would take up too much room here. In a sound philosophy of life it is of prime importance to realise their worth and know in how far their possession contributes to happiness, contentment, and a healthy life. There is scarcely a person who, if he were honest with himself, will admit that he is only happy and contented because he is rich. Happiness and contentment are not grounded in matter. Discontented people will never be made more content and happier through riches.

What actually is happiness in human life? It is the fulfilment of personal wishes, the granting or experiencing of what is good and pleasant beyond the impulses of personal will. However a sense of happiness can be problematic because often and very much later, one becomes aware of the fact that what was considered a stroke of luck was actually the cause of serious disadvantages in every respect.

But this realisation signifies great progress in the same way as the endurance of pain and suffering, of poverty and injustice, is later recognised as having been of great value for human or spiritual progress.

In the spiritual sphere man cannot aim too high to attain his goal; but only in relation to spirit and soul, not in relation to matter. All excessive and exaggerated demands on physical powers for the attainment of material advantages have disturbing and restricting effects on the spirit and primarily on the soul – the vital energy. What I say is not new, but it is necessary always to bear it in mind.

Do not let yourselves be led astray by material advantage and success. They are not the most important aspects for your progress! They may only be the means to the end, not the end in itself.

The most desirable goal is material success combined with a mature soul and spirit. If a person wishes to cultivate his soul and allow his spiritual existence free reign, he must know his limitations in material involvement.

This theme is the focal point if a healthy outlook in life is to be attained. I could express it this way: a healthy mental attitude requires the ability to find the correct measure in everything – the happy medium.

It is not easy for me to define this happy medium for I am freed from matter and may incline to scorn it or hold it in scant regard. But this is not right, for material life would be unthinkable without it.

It should be considered a gift from Divine Omnipotence, based on the principle that life must be lived in a community in which nobody should lay claim to more than he needs for his spiritual progress.

This should not be interpreted too literally, because spiritual progress in earthly existence also demands a healthy way of life and, consequently, the care and preservation of the material body.

With this I close for today. Next time I will write about how a person should learn to be aware of his life path in the material sphere.

The necessity of correct education and guidance.

I HAVE spoken about learning to find the right life path in order to be able to fulfil the tasks one has taken on for one's lifespan.

This seems much more difficult than it really is. It only requires the correct interpretation of the purpose of life and the willingness to progress to a more advanced stage. This is not dependent on material possessions as we have already said. Material contentment comes with the recognition of the value of spiritual progress. And this is the reason that correct guidance in childhood and youth is so important.

When adults will have reached the point that they recognise and understand this requirement and form their views on life according to these principles, real progress has been made.

Above all, there has to be the awareness that a child harbours a complete programme within it and therefore must be given the opportunity to have complete freedom of development. I cannot repeat this fact often enough. It is the main prerequisite for the correct rearing and treatment of a young spirit entity. Young, as I have already said, only in relation to the child's age, but not with regard to the spiritual maturity already attained.

In the first years of life a child's development is practically only physical. Natural law does not require it to make emotional and spiritual progress from day one in the material world. That it learns to speak and can see and hear belongs to material development as does everything that is part of material life and which we in the world beyond do not require for our existence and further evolution.

Therefore a distinction has also to be made between material development which includes the correct use of the five senses and progress in spiritual matters, which only begins much later. But this does not mean that knowledge which is brought along and the spiritual maturity which has been attained are not already evident to the beholder or teacher in early childhood.

To recognise this is really the task of parents and teachers if they are able to devote time to the maturing inner being. If material requirements do not allow parents the time and peace to devote themselves sufficiently to their offspring, it is their duty not to impede the free development of the child. They must be able to ensure that they can grant their children a physically healthy environment which furthers their growth. One will ask when the spiritual development, and therefore progress, can begin. This is, of course, difficult to say and not readily apparent to those around the child. The prerequisites are not created at the same time for everybody. We have already discussed the fact that every person is unique and both the spiritual and emotional development depends on various influences.

The ideal state of affairs is achieved when parents and teachers, initiated and convinced of the great correlations in the cosmos, are role models to their offspring and must not learn through their own mistakes where the requirements for a good education are to be sought.

If we therefore assume that a child has the best possible example imaginable in earthly circumstances, then we can expect that in its development will soon be an indication whether it has brought a certain calling to earth. It will not be difficult to guide the education and instruction in the required direction.

Education and instruction go hand in hand, but are very different elements in the life of the evolving person. Education mainly affects the soul; it is the guidance of vital energy and the will to God-given deeds and whatever is good and beautiful. Without this guidance, instruction, which is the technical schooling of the brain, will be quite one-sided if the maturity of the soul is not sufficiently strong to bring about the necessary balance.

If the child shows signs of firm principles and has an idea to which goal successful instruction should lead, then the ideal situation is evident at the very beginning.

To reach this goal, education must lead to the firm conviction that the purpose and reason for every achievement in the material sphere must be higher than material riches, power or even superiority over other people.

Community consciousness is what must be drummed into a child even if early on there are many opportunities to show it what this means through good examples set by its parents. It must learn that it lives and must live for the community. It is not necessary to teach it with many words and overwhelm it with warnings. This only leads to uncertainty in human relationships or creates a condition of resistance, and therefore a rejection of the well-meant words and deeds.

As soon as a child begins to learn the responsibilities of life, which is when it is forced to go to school and work, it already starts to ponder the virtue and usefulness of this exercise. The conclusions will be very diverse. In the case of a child who cannot or will not grasp the meaning of such instruction, the results will be nil. One dare not discourage very sensitive souls, but instead must constantly remind them of the results that will be theirs if they cheerfully fulfil the duties that have to be completed.

The reflections of a totally unselfconscious child on these matters contain a lot of truth. Conventional education is not always necessary for progress in the spiritual sense. If a child does not have the ambition to achieve great material results but is content with whatever it has achieved to date or what is being offered, then it will not understand the necessity for intellectual effort.

Civilisation and its ever increasing demands also makes it necessary to adapt to material progress, to achieve success in the material sense and acquire possessions that simply cannot be dispensed with if a healthy life style is to be maintained. So it is up to the teacher to convince the child with evidence that intellectual efforts are necessary.

After a few years the child, sensing a bigger programme within, will of its own accord feel where its path should lead and, availing itself of all the means offered it, begin to follow this path regardless of all the obstacles placed in its way.

Many people go to earth without the wish to make spiritual progress. They come – as I have already explained – only to enjoy worldly goods, thinking these are the absolute ultimate that the universe can offer them. These people need our loving attention so they can be taught modesty. Not by denying them worldly goods and possessions, but by convincing them how to use them properly, which is the only way they will find happiness in this sphere.

I must always make an effort to see things from an earthly point of view; when I do, I must admit that the desire for goods and possessions is justifiable, for they are the basis for independence and freedom in whatever career or occupation has been chosen.

This is why one ought to seek an occupation that is secure and should primarily serve the purpose of creating and preserving bodily comfort. This is the first phase of life's way that everybody must take if he wishes to be equipped for spiritual progress.

Knowledge and capability, or at least one of these attributes, is necessary to establish spiritual progress. Nobody can serve the community if he lives his life in an idle and ignorant fashion and seeks only to enjoy the benefits provided by others without making his personal contribution. It is always the community which helps a person to make spiritual progress. Everybody should dedicate work and knowledge to it if he wants to handle his earthly existence in a really happy and contented way.

But to be able to render the community good and useful service one must know how to assess and make use of purely material achievements. He who only thinks of himself and his own well-being will soon experience bitter disappointments. One must draw attention, once again, to the happy medium.

Every person is able to judge very accurately where the limits of what is necessary and what is superfluous lie. It only requires goodwill to remain within these limits. But once a person has established the correct measure in material exigencies, a benevolent power will guide him to marvellous spiritual matters. Nobody who prepares himself for this will be excluded. And now spiritual development begins to show quite definite progress; it is not visible to those around, but can be felt because of the greater harmony in the person concerned.

Faulty education and, above all, man's totally erroneous conception of the blessing of wealth in the material world, only allows this realisation to mature more or less strongly in advanced years. This leads to the condescending conclusion that a positive attitude towards the community is a foible of old age instead of recognising that the way to such a God-given attitude to life is actually hard and stony.

But if good examples point the child on its way in its infancy, people will achieve this maturity much earlier. With this, enough for today.

The aura, kinship on earth and in the world beyond.

TODAY I want to speak of matters which are particularly important for the understanding of the correlations with other-worldly rules and laws.

In life it does not matter whether a person has the advantage of being held in high esteem by others. Appearances are often deceptive. People are frequently incorrect and unsure in their judgement of fellow men.

I have already pointed out that everybody, in accordance with his spiritual maturity and harmony, has an aura. It must be understood that the spirit entity, which in the other world consists purely of light rays, is also apparent in earthly existence, although it is invisible to the material eye. Only spiritual sight permits recognition of the aura on earth. Very few persons on earth are allowed to have this spiritual sight. It is not bestowed arbitrarily but according to eternal laws. But even if these rays are not visible in the material sphere – for I must always consider the prevailing circumstances – it is an indisputable fact that they affect the environment. According to the maturity of the spirit entity, this will be more – or less – beneficial.

Exerting an effect is not synonymous with receiving and feeling it. Not everybody is in a position or able to allow these rays to affect him or to be aware of them and react to them spiritually or emotionally. Responding to such an effect requires reflection and a certain emotional willingness to receive it; even, I would say, a degree of passiveness. Also in these matters everything proceeds according to hard and fast rules. But for the practical knowledge of human nature it is very important that in some way or other one is in a position to establish if the environment in which one finds oneself and the people with whom one wishes to have a close, if not the closest relationship, have auras compatible with one's own; that is to say if they are similar, if they are kindred.

This is the crux of today's theme. What is kinship? In earthly life and materially considered it is a physical similarity, a lineal descent from a father and a mother. Man and woman are not necessarily related to each other before marriage. In material life it is not desirable as the findings of many hundred years have shown. In earthly life kinship is the result of physical reproduction. That the father and mother also establish a kinship through marriage is understandable and, within the framework of civilisation, absolutely necessary. But, I might add, this is not genuine kinship, only an affinitive relationship.

Only earthly laws demand a relational bond between man and woman, but not the eternal, otherworldly laws that govern everlasting life.

This is why, among primitive peoples, polygamy is taken for granted. The primitive instinct of these people tells them that an inner and real relationship between marriage partners is lacking.

It is only after departure from the material world that this theory is seen to be correct and is accepted because only then does a person see the aura of the partner he was bound to, be it that he is still on earth or has also reached the other-worldly sphere. I had to ascertain that my wife had an aura that was completely different to mine. Therefore our relationship came to an end with earthly death. As our marriage was childless, even this link in the material sense was lost to us, although it could only have culminated in spiritual responsibility because for children the concept of relationship falls away the moment the material bond, the body, disintegrates or is abandoned.

I have already drawn attention to the fact that the spirit entity and the soul are indivisible and cannot be inherited through birth. I have also explained that at the birth of a child the spirit entity is incarnated quite independently of the physical prerequisites which, of course, are to be understood according to the material point of view.

But it must be taken into consideration that incarnation is established in accordance with eternal, divine laws and is not arbitrary or accidental. One so often talks of similar mental abilities, of general similarity of character, between parents and children. From this one draws the conclusion that the children's temperament has simply been inherited and the parents are responsible for all their good or bad habits. This is very natural, but in no way correct.

Kinship in the true meaning of the word is a bond in the spiritual world for eternity; it is unity and complement to the coveted state of perfection.

It is determined in advance for every spirit entity. I have already pointed out that this state of perfection cannot be attained by a spirit entity on its own. Every state of perfection requires a complement, a duality.

This principle also exists in earthly life, but its conception is very material and therefore full of mistakes and incorrect connotations.

Marriage, in earthly existence is seldom – very seldom – made in heaven and is the true complement in the spiritual sense. Nevertheless it is God-given if good resolutions and pure thoughts and wishes form the basis of the union of two people. The saying that marriages are made in heaven is correct, but is falsely interpreted by people and particularly by the Church.

I hardly think that a good priest who knows he is marrying two people who are entering into a marriage contract for purely material reasons, greed and cupidity can be convinced that such a partnership is worth a divine blessing or that they could even demand such a blessing.

I can imagine that many an honest clergyman feels revulsion in his breast and would rather say: "Put aside these lies and hypocrisy. I cannot give God's blessing to such a union." He could give it with the indication that this marriage in all probability was not God-given or that there had to be doubts about it, but that Divine Omnipotence holds his hand over all those who really try to find the right path. It should be more of a call to show oneself worthy of a blessing rather than to stress that God had validated this marriage for all time.

Now the question has to be answered: when such a marriage is made in heaven and becomes reality, is it consciously identifiable in the earthly sphere?

It is determined according to eternal laws at which point in time a union of duality is allowed and scheduled. There is no criterion for such a union; by this I mean that no particular spiritual maturity of both spirit entities destined for each other is necessary. If two such really kindred souls find themselves in earthly existence, it can be that they are united as really good friends, marriage partners or father and son. The bond between them will always be harmonious. The people around them who look on benevolently, will be able to feel the unison. They themselves will not be able to establish it fully; this is the great secret of our earthly existence.

Great tests can also be linked to the earthly association of twin souls. One of them can help the other to fulfil his tasks and enhance his spiritual development. Twin souls will never hinder the progress of their partners, even though, in the earthly sense, discord and unequal standards sometimes seem to disturb progress and well-being.

I mentioned in my foreword that it is really not easy to reconcile the concepts on earth with those in the world beyond. In the other world not every spirit entity is in a position to establish where his twin soul is to be found. It is considered an act of particular grace if one is permitted to find one's perfect complement. Progress is then enhanced and double strength animates the souls who are permitted to take the right road together. This is why I will not say that such a situation is not possible in earthly life; the difference is only that on earth the timespan of the tests and the improvement and progress is hampered by material obstacles.

This is the value of earthly existence; that man, of his own free will and power of thought, must learn where the right path begins and how he must tread it. In the world beyond all obstacles are removed. Only goodwill and confidence in Divine Omnipotence, which is available to everybody and is recognised by every true searcher, is needed to progress and become richer in knowledge and wisdom.

Advanced spirits who are allowed to find their twin souls make unbelievable progress. Less developed souls and spirit entities can also be united with their twin souls, but they will be separated again if they prove to be unworthy of this grace and fail to recognise the extreme value of the union. They will also be separated again if the goodwill for harmony is lacking or the craving for material possessions is dominant. It is the same in the world beyond, where recognition is afforded through spiritual sight. With this thought I would like to end this chapter, but we will revert to the subject again in a different context.

A comparison between earthly life and existence in the world beyond. The circle of scholars.

TODAY I will begin to explain the differences that exist between the earthly conception of life after death and the actual circumstances in so far as they are significant for earthly life and the further development of the earthly race.

Peoples' ideas of conditions in the world beyond are governed by their earthly imaginative abilities and are in accordance with events and experiences in this material world. It is therefore quite wrong to make comparisons where pre-conditions are so totally different in every respect.

We already know something about this; mainly that in the world beyond matter – in the earthly sense – is unnecessary. I say "in the earthly sense" – because, after all, a ray of light is substance, although admittedly one that cannot be held and is not bound to space.

This is where the difference begins. For life on earth this substance, light, is absolutely necessary and not only in relation to brightness, daylight, and sight. There are also rays which man does not regard as light rays because he cannot see them, but which nevertheless fall under this heading according to otherworldly laws. They are indispensable for human existence and yet people are unaware of them. But why do some want to know so much about life after death when humanity has still so much to discover about life on earth.

We must always be aware of the fact that the circle of vision and the powers of comprehension of material people are so limited that they cannot think beyond their ideas of space and time, of light and darkness, as they know it in their world.

Whatever exists on the material plane and promotes life, development and earthly progress, forms peoples' imaginative abilities in a very restricted fashion. Man is not able to formulate concepts and doctrines for events and particular kinds of life which do not exist on earth.

We here in the world beyond do not need food and care to further our development as the earthly body does, yet we too enjoy an increase of strength in a way that cannot be conveyed in earthly terms. There have often been attempts to communicate and explain this. But they are only a rendition, a very vague effort to make these otherworldly events understandable. Such communications have therefore been relegated by earthly people to the realms of fairy tales.

Genuine understanding or belief in extra-terrestrial forms of life is therefore lost and all serious communications which should benefit mankind and its progress are banished from the sphere of serious research. But this is of no use for the development and progress of man, for the attitude that everything which is neither tangible nor visible for mankind is unreal and belongs to the realm of fantasy is also unhealthy and restrictive.

Man must also have the courage to concern himself seriously with those matters that are not so easy to understand, and be prepared to study them. But it is certainly not a task for everybody. Rather it is the responsibility of science to investigate the correct and natural principles of the proper conception of life and make it understandable to the general community as a whole.

The prevailing natural laws do not call for the masses to worry themselves with the great correlations, just as they are not concerned whether their religious education, be it in the Christian or any other faith, is proven or not. They follow the instructions of the Church without contradiction, even allowing themselves to be punished and finding that quite fair and proper. So it must be possible to open up new paths. It must be possible to convince them that all knowledge about the world beyond that is important for earthly life forms the basis for their development and existence. Let us not forget that everybody is basically good. It must also be possible to make him understand a correct philosophy of life and realise how advantageous it is.

I am not trying to say that a new religion should be created overnight. The Church with its existing infrastructure and trained men must change its views, overcome and eliminate its mistakes and open itself to the new knowledge. There is already a big movement afoot, not only in the Christian religion – or better said in the Christian confessions – but in all other religions on earth.

But what precisely should be taught and learned in religious instruction? As far as life within the framework of earthly civilisation is concerned, this is known and must no longer be explained. I want only to speak of what people should know about what awaits them, what lies before them, what the continuation of earthly existence is and which goal they should bear in mind.

For many of those who are not particularly advanced in their spiritual development it is enough to know that a happy existence can be expected for all who have fulfilled their duties in this world with goodwill and to the best of their ability. But the aspirant must know about the correlations and be protected from mistakes that could obstruct and delay his progress.

This is why I say that it is necessary to see life in the material world in its proper perspective; do not overestimate matter and consider that only those people who are proficient in accumulating material possessions are dynamic.

What is important for the progress of mankind in spiritual matters is primarily to pay attention to and cultivate whatever is continued in the world beyond. Recognition of the fact that one cannot take material possessions with one and store them for another lifetime has increasingly shown proof of their lack of value. Great wealth often characterises the pure materialist whose possessions leave him no time for spiritual matters and the care of his soul and spirit.

This is why it is often a far greater test for earthly people to be more than amply blessed with worldly possessions than the cross-section of mankind.

I would like to indicate the guidelines for earthly life and what is equally valid and has its continuation in the world beyond if it is built on a good foundation or even one that has been only moderately developed on earth.

Only the soul and the spirit entity carry over the achievements of the material world into the world beyond. The soul, as the seat of the emotions, should learn to feel what is right and good in every situation in life and so, together with the community, seek and find goodness, love, kindness, readiness to help and understanding friendship.

In the mental field, it is free will that must aspire to what is fair and right, to knowledge and higher achievements in order to fulfil tasks for the benefit of the community. This will be in accordance with the way a person has been brought up and educated. By striving to be worthy of his calling, he must endeavour to reach his goal, or at least bring it nearer.

And if one were to ask how such knowledge and abilities perfected in earthly life are utilised in the world beyond, I can make this very clear, even for material understanding.

The school of life does not end with departure from the earth. It continues exactly where it stopped here.

First of all, I must explain that although we do not have physical bodies, due to our spiritual eyesight in our radiatory condition, we appear as human beings. I will explain it in terms of my own experience. I came over and was received by my good guide after I had accepted that I was no longer living in the material world. Our bodies, however, are not as they were in the final stages on earth but young and in the full bloom of life because all physical suffering has disappeared. I came over in full possession of my vital energy and hardly needed time to build it up to a normal, healthy level.

My only drawback was my doubt about the existence of the world beyond. While I continued to believe that I was only dreaming, I could not enter the other-worldly realm. But then I came upon a circle of scholars and subsequently the company of those who represent medical science and strive to do justice to the high calling. In contrast to the material world I was given a most cordial reception. To begin with I held myself aloof; I saw and heard what my colleagues who had crossed over before me discussed, but could not participate in the talks.

When I write of "seeing" and "hearing" it must not be taken literally. We do not speak because we lack an organ of speech; we read thoughts whenever we wish to, without necessarily letting the person concerned know that we are doing so.

A session of our circle will not be readily understood according to earthly concepts, but the impact of our learned meetings is of great value because mistakes conveyed by spoken words do not occur. Soon I was included in the circle and could make known my thoughts, which I offered for discussion. The recognition of the correlations with the world beyond made a strong impression on me, and I began to test the accuracy of the doctrines I advocated in earthly life. I have related some of this in previous chapters. There is much that still has to be investigated and made clear.

The difference in the communal work here and on earth lies in the fact that here there is true, selfless teamwork, whereas on earth the keynote is the drive for a higher position and pre-eminence over others, even in a scientific profession. This is detrimental to progress and impedes many a superior talent and many an ability to achieve something great for mankind.

Here everything is for the benefit of the community; it is directed to a common goal. Everybody supports everybody else to the best of his ability. It must be taken into account that our scientific work does not need a material basis. Where matter is the prerequisite, the struggle for existence, for rank and for position is unavoidable.

Nevertheless in this field the care and promotion of a calling should be the primary consideration and the way ought to be smoothed for whoever shows the greatest abilities and talents. The acquisition of a doctor's degree by no means signifies the end of school. It really only begins when one realises what a long path still lies ahead. In this respect the limitation of the earthly horizon is a blessing for humanity because every serious-minded researcher would despair if he realised that science was still in its early infancy and further from, rather than nearer, a more or less satisfactory level.

We here see quite a number of things that we would like to tell people, but we may not because the necessary standard in earthly thought has not yet been attained. As I have said, everything is arranged in accordance with exact rules. We are not allowed to pass on information if the time is not ripe. We do not decide this; the infinite laws of the cosmos make the decision. We here can recognise their rigid, irrevocable, logical sequence, but they cannot be understood by the people living on earth.

The further, therefore, that man progresses in his earthly development, the higher the level of the circle that he will enter here. Knowledge and learning are not a part of this; they just happened to be the criterion of the circle to which I belong. What decides the level of the circle is the development of the personality, of the character and the proof furnished of this. In all areas of earthly life achievements and good deeds must be accomplished and substantiated. It is of absolutely no consequence where man renders his services in material life. The tasks set for him to aid his spiritual progress will be brought to him. If he were to know this, the results would be doubtful because then his will would have been consciously directed to this fact and to a certain extent forced by consciousness and knowledge of the results to follow.

A task must be undertaken and brought to fruition through free will as a test of oneself without any outside influence, otherwise the result is meaningless. The mainspring of every action must be a general striving to progress and reach a higher level through good deeds.

We have yet to examine other areas related to the world beyond and the results of good or bad mastering of life's lessons. Enough for today.

The calling to be a teacher and its further development in the fourth dimension.

YESTERDAY I spoke about the circle of scholars, their tasks and their aspirations to progress. But I do not want to create the impression that a scholar must only seek progress in the scientific sphere. If he really wants to achieve something of value for the community, he has to form his character and correct and perfect his concept of life in equal measure.

What a person does in addition to his calling to science and how he behaves towards the community are not without consequence. Many, or most, scientists and scholars make a great mistake. Because of their superior knowledge they consider themselves above the crowd and look down on it with condescension.

Peoples' judgement still stems from very false criteria and is seldom correct. This too is principally because of dependence on matter and must change if one is to make a worthy judgement of one's fellow men.

But now let us look at another circle which, as in earthly life, continues in the world beyond and offers people the possibility of making good what they neglected to do on earth, whether or not they were responsible for it. This is the position of educator and teacher. Not everybody who chooses the vocation of teacher in life was called to it. When he comes over to the other world he often realises that he made the wrong choice and lacked talent for this profession. But this is not serious because existing basic elements which have nothing to do with the career of teaching can be utilised in this profession too. It may be a purely technical or manual gift which would have made greater strides in the technical field, but in conjunction with the education of youngsters could help them to progress. But very often, the ability which could have been used for the benefit of the community, is not, and the necessary prerequisites to become a teacher are lacking. This causes the teacher a great deal of internal conflict because he is aware of the fact that he lacks talent for the calling and the pupils also realise that they have an unsuitable guide before them.

Therefore, there should be the opportunity of changing careers without great material loss. This would certainly be the case were outside influences not so obstructive. But people who realise that they have failed seldom find a suitable solution. On the other hand, if a person is born to be a teacher, then, like the scientist, he will be true to his calling and progress along the road that he trod in an earlier life.

Just as the representatives of medical science are able to pin-point – once they have left the material world – in which matters they have made mistakes and where they have based their work on incorrect doctrines, so too does the teacher see where his attitude towards the people entrusted to him was incorrect and where it was in accordance with God's will a blessing and for the benefit of his charges.

In every area it depends on whether there is goodwill to recognise this oneself and accept instruction. As a scholar stubbornly immersed in earthly science – I mean undeveloped science – refuses to see that he has achieved nothing in his earthly existence but has only erred, so it is in all other careers. A teacher must, above all, acquire a good, healthy philosophy of life if he wishes to be a good, clever, and fair leader for youth. Here too recognition of mistakes is a prerequisite for progress; for one's own as well as for those who are affected by it. How different the opinion in schools is today about the value of a good education. A teacher who is called, and many are without knowing it, will continue to work for his progress after he leaves the material world. He will take pains to develop as a good example and, after thorough schooling from his good guide, return to serve the poor people and help them along the difficult path of development.

But often he lands on the path of materialism and all good resolutions will be obscured and repressed because bad examples do not permit his blueprint and his good abilities to come to fruition. In this circle it is very difficult to find the right way because only highly developed spirits can do so. So in this respect too we must show much patience until the ideal state of affairs is attained.

If, in the same way we examine the calling of a mother and father, we have to admit that the problem is exactly the same. A woman who believes herself to have been the best of mothers and to have fulfilled her calling, very often realises that she is still very far removed from perfection. To be a mother does not only mean to be a wife in marriage and a parent, but every woman who has to rear and care for her own child is included in this category. Very few mothers are truly called and fully master the task. Once again the disturbing influences of the material world are the cause of many a failure, although great progress has been made. We will still have a lot to say about the duties of a mother.

In the world beyond there is a school for mothers where there is instruction and advancement. Here mothers continue their activities even though they are not with their own children, as on earth. For here birth is unnecessary. Spirit entities who had to end their lives on earth in early childhood and have not yet understood their transition into the world beyond are in need of motherly care and are placed under the guidance of good mother spirits.

It can be argued that even in a small child there is a complete spirit which has only to develop in the material sense in order to fulfil the programme it has brought along. This is correct, but is not quite in agreement with development in the universe according to the infinite laws. The spirit of an immature person which returns to the world beyond again must continue to develop the maturity it achieved here. It is easier to do so here because all material obstacles fall away. But it has to go through the same stages of development as a child in the material sphere.

It is together with these child spirits that mothers receive instruction and learn how to guide the youngster. Of course, this is under our supervision and control. I want to stress that motherhood is the vocation of these women. In their next incarnation they will carry deep within them the knowledge they have acquired in the world beyond.

Comparing the ideas about education of a few hundred years ago with those of today, inspires confidence in the future. Great progress has been made in this field.

There is one more career to mention. It is that of the spiritual adviser – the priest. I have already mentioned how difficult it is for a good priest to realise in how many matters he was wrongly trained. It is easier to rectify a mistake resulting from personal reflection than those which have been absorbed with complete conviction from the teaching of a great dogma in which total reliance has been placed. Many, therefore, persist in error with total belief and there is no way to abandon such views. This is why we have already mentioned that many communications from the world beyond must not be accepted as irrefutably correct because they are based on belief and not on knowledge. High dignitaries of the Church who lived in the material world many hundreds of years ago, still refuse to return to it. They have gathered their priests around them and are firmly convinced they have to continue acting in the same way as they did on earth.

However, this clinging to mistaken beliefs in many matters is not serious. These are errors that can be forgiven and will certainly be eliminated one day. The development of character, the harmony of spirit and soul and the honest endeavours to make progress along the path to truth are much more important.

This is why, as I have already said, many a little cleric is far above an important priest or a high Church dignitary who has been canonised.

I am not allowed to discuss the nature of their errors. My narrative has to make clear how life continues in the world beyond and develops according to law; always progressing in the positive sense with the aim of making life in the material world more suitable for advanced development. Even if it is only step by step, it must be admitted that there is progress in this direction. With this, enough for today.

The conception of progress in spirit life.

TODAY I want to discuss how people should imagine progress in spirit life, and what this phrase should mean to them. We have spoken so much about progress, but a complete understanding requires a definition of how it is to be recognised.

Life is full of errors. But we make progress and attain higher stages of development because we recognise our errors and admit that we have taken the wrong path. By and large we are really only small, unimportant and ignorant beings who know less about living than can be imagined.

Dependent on matter – I speak as though I still live in the earthly world as time and again in material lives I made mistakes and took wrong paths – we have not grasped the true meaning of life. To recognise the true correlations in the cosmos and adapt oneself to them is one of our greatest tasks.

But to attain this ability, this state of clairvoyance, we have to pass a number of tests and graduate from many schools of life. It is not clairvoyance as people on earth understand the word – the ability to look into the future and see events in advance that must surely come to pass without any connection with circumstances today. The clairvoyance to which I refer is the distinct recognition of existing correlations, the correct interpretation of the purpose of earthly life. It is not only with intellect and faith that this task must be understood to be the basis of progress; one's entire being, soul and spirit has to be filled with it. Only then will the correct attitude to matters terrestrial and extra-terrestrial be determined and progress be assured.

We must always be aware of the fact that everything that happens to us in earthly existence is according to a significant set pattern. We must never assume we have been exposed to pure chance. Based on this fundamental truth we will consciously and with good intent direct our will in an intelligent, clever, kind-hearted manner to all tasks and not care whether they have proved useful or successful in the material sense.

To perform all tasks with the conviction that they are a small contribution towards the building up of our personal selves, our personalities, or that they are for the benefit of our fellow men, is fulfilment for people, because only such an attitude makes them happy, free and content. Free, because imperfectly, incorrectly fulfilled or accomplished tasks result in inner dependence which burdens the soul and spirit, and continually impedes the expression of life.

This is easy to imagine. We have all experienced such situations. As children we had to learn that a small blunder – a broken window, bad schoolwork, a fight with friends – dampened our pleasure and enjoyment, and often took away all the energy we needed to accomplish something which otherwise would easily have been done. Our appetite decreases when a mistake, which we have to admit to, weighs us down. In these small matters, for, seen from here they are infinitely small causes and effects, we must, however, begin to find the right approach, learn to gauge the meaning of all happenings and in honest appraisal not resign oneself to a destructive indictment of our errors with the viewpoint that we cannot do better.

We must draw the one and only correct conclusion: the error has been created to further our progress and impress upon us the conscious knowledge that we have to set our sights higher; that we have to improve and make good where we have failed once or many times. We must always look at ourselves objectively; contemplate and criticise ourselves honestly. This is the way to progress.

But to do this we have to judge our existing strength accurately, whether it be the spiritual or the physical. To be aware of one's own limitations is an essential prerequisite for a perfect achievement. Not everybody who studies a branch of science can become a great scholar. Not every composer, however talented, can aspire to the level of Mozart or Bach. He is well aware of his limitations, but is either too modest to assert his position or overestimates his abilities and demands more from himself than he is able to give.

Herein lies the great task for everybody. Do I have the ability to achieve this or the other goal? Have I set my sights high enough and utilised my available powers to the best of my ability?

Only after the end of material existence does one often realise that one has not adhered to the correct life line and has achieved either too little or something completely wrong. When rearing young people, educators must strive to recognise the life line, the present course in life, bearing in mind the world beyond, both in the past and in the future.

That which has been brought from an earlier life manifests itself in the attitude to the present life, to the type of contact one has with one's fellow men and to the endeavours to make progress.

I will give a concrete example of this. A young man who is already kind and helpful in school, certainly had a calling in earlier incarnations to a way of life based on these virtues. During the years that the boy is entrusted to them, his teachers must be able to establish to which career these virtues incline and if he has the necessary mental abilities for the work in question. It is not always easy to establish this because, as we know, numerous outside influences obscure the real picture.

Serious work in this direction is already being undertaken, and psychological research can be credited with numerous successes. But the aspects under which these opinions occur are not always perfect or correct. A young person in his formative years absorbs a lot through example and education, thereby repressing his true nature and, perhaps, his calling. Then, very often, in later years there is inner conflict and discontent with the chosen career because he realises that progress is at a standstill and almost atrophied as the fundamental prerequisites are lacking. This is the time when a so-called secondary occupation comes into being. For the progress of the person – or rather his spirit entity – it is much more important than the main career.

I have already mentioned this, but want to emphasise once again that people must strive to find ways and means of recognising and fostering the preordained achievements within community life on earth in a suitable manner.

As I have said so often, this necessitates the correct assessment of matter. When choosing an occupation or a career, the accumulation of matter must not be the ultimate goal. At present, matter is still the biggest obstacle to the way ahead. Conquering it will clear the path for everybody who honestly seeks to make progress.

When can matter be considered conquered? The obvious answer is, "When we possess an adequate amount." The answer is not incorrect, but needs a slight adjustment and it is this: we will possess an adequate amount when worldly goods have been apportioned and put to use in such a way that all inhabitants of the earth receive sufficient for their existence and nobody needs to avail himself of more than he requires for the healthy maintenance of his life.

People would be amazed if they could look a few hundred years into the future and see how sensible mankind had become in relation to the enjoyment of worldly goods compared with the squandermania that presently exists.

The attitude towards matter together with the spread of infinite truth and the recognition of the correlations with the universe will automatically bring about a recovery of a kind that would hardly be credited now. With this, enough for today.

The aura of fellow human beings and the correct attitude towards them.

TODAY I will write about the manner in which people should focus their thoughts on their fellow men to achieve a suitable contact, a correct opinion, a favourable attitude and so on.

I have already mentioned that everybody has an aura. It is a valuable possession, and of greater consequence for material life than one would like to believe.

Everything that influences daily life and spiritual progress is significant, whether in the positive or negative sense. As I have already explained, it is important to feel the aura of the people around, to identify and investigate it spiritually with understanding.

This is not always possible at the first encounter because, in addition to the aura of a person, there are other powers at work which can neither be seen nor directly felt.

Warmth and cold influence our nervous system and, according to their intensity, produce a feeling of well-being or discomfort.

If one wishes to investigate the aura of a person, judgement should not be passed after only one encounter. Only very few people are sufficiently receptive for their souls to be touched by the rays generated by an aura. In addition, it requires a certain positive passiveness and peace, a benevolent attitude towards the other person.

If thoughts are negatively influenced before one even meets the person because one has heard or read bad things about him, then particular independence of judgement will be necessary in order not to be influenced by this.

If one wishes to be aware of a person's aura – to feel harmony or antipathy – one must, above all, remain tranquil and objective and allow the person to exert his influence. It is not easy to explain this condition; one must try to detach oneself from the individual in question, not concentrate one's thoughts intensely on him, but create an atmosphere of peace and restraint to allow his character to come through.

As the doctor averts his eyes from his patient when he wants him to come out of his shell and gives him complete freedom to expand his thoughts, so it should be in daily life in every single instance. How many misunderstandings would be spared in this way.

People mostly make the mistake of thinking with their interlocutor when he begins to speak. What they do is think ahead of what he is saying and thereby come to a wrong conclusion. It is exactly the same with the feeling of a person's radiation. It touches the soul subconsciously and according to the condition of the latter, transmits the sensation. But if the soul of the recipient is disturbed, it will only transmit weakly or not at all; it will feel itself weighed down by the radiation it has received and will either reject or make only minimal contact with it.

This is why individuals with healthy souls make contact easily and are readily accepted, whereas people with sick souls or those full of inhibitions are disliked. Reciprocity of radiations will not take place and their harmonious mergings are prevented.

One should not seek to judge people or at least not come to final conclusions if one is depressed or one's spiritual or emotional frame of mind is low. Any personal feelings of inferiority cloud a clear, honest and objective thought pattern. Involuntarily one inclines to an incorrect judgement. The disappointment is bitter when one realises that one has made a mistake.

But let us assume that a person is quite able and predestined to absorb the radiations of his fellow men and can assess them properly. He will allow the people around to make their impression on him quite passively. He consciously rejects whatever could cloud or influence his judgement and inwardly withdrawn, if only for a short moment, test the effect he feels. Everybody can sense this effect when he meets with another person and establish whether it creates a pleasant or uneasy atmosphere.

Time and again in daily life we say that such and such a person is disagreeable or unpleasant. We are happy to meet somebody who is compatible, even though we have little time to chat and are impatient and extremely uneasy if an incompatible person comes along, despite the fact that we have enough time to spare.

Few people bother to investigate the reasons for such diverse behaviour and yet they are the surest signs of acceptance or rejection of the rays that have been received.

Just as one seeks a state of passiveness for the care of one's soul and withdraws inwardly to allow only the good powers of the universe entrance, so too, in order to receive the pure, unclouded recognition of the nature of one's fellow men, of their character and spiritual maturity, one must place oneself on a sound and receptive basis. Just as a child opens its arms quite unselfconsciously to catch a thrown ball, so too must a person open himself to the rays sent out to him. But just as the child must make a grab for the ball and close its arms around it to hold it, so the person must – at the right moment – hold fast the impression, not letting it ricochet off his soul, but sealing it inwardly and allowing his spirit to decide whether something good or bad has touched his soul.

If the radiation is accepted as being good, it still does not mean that we are in agreement with this person on all matters .

Who is in a position to make a decision as to whether another person is better or worse? By this I mean inferior to oneself. This is a weighty matter. We have yet to write about it in relation to character formation and judgement. Our decision, and I consciously use the word "our" because these basic rules also apply in the world beyond and can only be in accordance with the level of our own spiritual maturity, will therefore not be irrefutably correct in all cases. We shall certainly be able to see that a person of advanced emotional and spiritual maturity is superior to us, even though a mistake in the earthly sphere is possible and understandable because we can only appraise the intensity of the radiation with spiritual sight.

This is the school to which earthly man is sent in order to advance the development of his spirit in this area through unselfish, personal judgement, recognition of the possibilities and the acquisition of the ability to find the right path by his own efforts.

We have already discussed the fact that man cannot progress alone, I mean spiritually, on account of the eternal laws of nature. Because, as we already know, it is not just a matter of living life after a fashion in the material world without making any great mistakes – mistakes in the purely material sense.

Life must progress in the community for the community. And to tread this path correctly, a great deal of knowledge of human nature is needed. I will explain again what I mean by this although we have already discussed it. I would say it is the endeavour to feel oneself into the psyche of people, to find the correct relationship, the right art of living with the community; to be its good, honest and benevolent servant.

Only when we are prepared to serve our fellow men with a pure heart, with real pleasure at being able to assist them, then practical knowledge of human nature is of value. To be able to determine that somebody makes one uncomfortable, gets in one's way or is without use, is pointless and not conducive to progress.

We must certainly have the possibility of avoiding, or endeavouring to avoid, association with less developed people, but only in so far as we do not have to conform to their level. To help them to progress, to try to combat their mistakes, is the task which I have often referred to.

We learn much from the mistakes of others. For the more advanced person many a subject is only clearly defined in terms of good and evil, and right and wrong, once he is familiar with all the powers and energies that influence the development of mankind.

Today I have only written the introduction to what I still have to say about knowledge of human nature. There are many characteristics, both good and bad, which must be recognised in order to establish a complete picture of a person. More about this next time.

Knowledge of human nature and human contact in professional life.

YESTERDAY I spoke of the necessity to receive the radiation of a person willingly if one has the wish to learn about his character and his influence on oneself or the people around.

This is not always necessary; it would be pointless to test every encounter. But in many a situation in life it is extremely important as often progress, sometimes even a career, depends on it. If in professional life you have a superior with whom you are on the best of terms, apart from your qualifications for this activity, your work will give you pleasure and you happily do everything possible to give him satisfaction. This would not be the case if there was obvious dislike. But where does this come from, if material causes – by this I mean financial satisfaction and the right employment – leave nothing to be desired? It is simply a case of personal dislike. In this case there is a divergence in radiations; the two people bound together by work find no inner contact and yet it is very important for both of them to do so in order to achieve results.

This is why everybody who seeks a subordinate position in a professional occupation must carefully consider whether it would give him pleasure to work for his superiors in the company. Not only for the financial remuneration; it is the least important aspect, even if people today still regard their wages as the yardstick for the quality of a position. Fortunately, not everybody is like this, for it would be pitiful and hopeless if really everybody only considered his wallet, and his work and the pleasure it gave him was unimportant and secondary.

How many people renounce material advantages and pleasure because their work, which they love above all, is more important, even though they only eke out a scanty living from it! The world calls this unsound idealism. The general opinion is that these people can be considered incompetent and stupid.

Quite the contrary. They are the upholders, the real champions of a correct philosophy of life, and should be more highly prized and respected than the greedy people and so-called greats who use their material success as a sign-board to make a name for themselves.

When dealing with the study of human nature much attention is to be paid to the distinction between appearances and truth. It is, as I have already pointed out, the most difficult task in earthly existence to recognise what is good, genuine, valuable and necessary for progress. Not everybody is in a position to do this. Bitter disappointments are often the prerequisite for the effort to seek the truth and avoid appearance.

Practically every person comes to the conclusion in the course of his life that despite many so-called friends he is alone and cannot find the people who would satisfy him in every respect. No wonder, for hardly anybody considers which requirements must be fulfilled in order to establish the right contact.

Time and again I come back to the same point of departure for the path that has to be taken. The material background must be cast aside and the frame that blocks a clear view of the picture removed. It is not material success that indicates value, or at least only in the rarest of cases.

If one wants to know whether a person belongs to an advanced level, one should consider his views on life in relation to his surroundings and himself, or better said, with respect to his concept of himself.

People who are so taken with themselves that they believe they are a cut above the average and do not need the community or outside influence to make progress are, as we have said, egocentric, only concerned with their own well-being and without consideration for the requirements that must be fulfilled in order to live in peace and harmony with their surroundings. Such individuals one recognises immediately; they are only bothered with their own importance and ignore the wishes or the consideration necessary towards those around them.

Should one wish to test a person in this matter, ask him a trivial question. He will either not answer it because the answer embarrasses him or he will reply in a way that shows he can only think in relation to himself. The word "I" will have precedence, and it is very clear that he regards his opinion as irrefutable. He will brook no contradiction and give no indication of trying to adapt or project himself into the other person's mind.

Of course, such a judgement is not always possible at the first encounter. The prevailing frame of mind, attitude and purpose of a discussion can deceive and give rise to a wrong opinion.

A manager, for instance, who deliberately is extremely friendly towards his staff, makes a first impression of benevolence, kindness, unselfishness and generosity. But the insincerity soon shines through, because real goodness and charity cannot be feigned; conversely, it also cannot be denied.

A personal, truthful, honest contact to staff is the most important prerequisite for trusting, successful co-operation. It is not true that in big organisations such a goal is unattainable. No matter how great the distance is between management and staff, it is never so great that it cannot be bridged. This is what is known as a good atmosphere in a concern, and is created when the employer or the manager allows a good, positive radiation to be felt consciously and with goodwill. Those in a position of power who consider that their status places them so far above their staff that any contact with them is unnecessary because they have satisfactory wages will not enjoy their great success long. Few employees are so materialistic that they enjoy their work only on account of their wages.

It is not without reason that one wonders why the morale of a business is low, despite high wages. The morale of an organisation is not raised by offering better financial remuneration. This comes from a human approach, a slow bridging of the gap through respect and regard for every person with whom one comes in contact.

In my dealings with people during my earthly existence, I always adhered to the principle that everybody has the same rights, the same claim to respect and consideration as I wished for myself. I never received it in the same measure that I gave it, but that is of no importance.

The reaction to a mark of esteem showed me the character of the person in question – often in an unmistakeable fashion. If either the man or the woman – the sex was unimportant in a study of this kind – was prominent in the material sense, I could very soon tell if the person was modest or if he accepted my deference as a matter of course.

Such matters are milestones in practical knowledge of human nature. But the study must be made with great care, because often an honourable remark is met with insincere modesty. But a trained eye and ear soon established the difference between appearance and reality.

This was a small excerpt of practical knowledge of human nature. I say "practical" because theoretical observation only of striking characteristics is worthless if reciprocity and common interest does not result from it. Knowledge of human nature ought to contribute to honest and profitable relationships between people; it should not be an exercise to establish interesting observations on the one hand and condemnation on the other. A way must be found to make use of better characteristics that one observes in others, and to help others to emulate the assets or spiritual characteristics one has achieved. Only in this way will a peaceful mankind strive in unison to promote its progress and avoid appearance and deception. Even though this will not come about overnight, we can look to the future with confidence and await a better mankind – one striving to find the right way. With this, enough for today.

The study of influences on the emotional life.

TODAY I will begin to point out the rudiments that must, of necessity, be understood in order to make a correct diagnosis when the influences of the earthly sphere, previously referred to, have been established with measuring instruments and other mechanical tests.

As already stated, the doctor has to examine and test an area for which there are no tangible reactions and measured values. This is the purely psychic and mental area. Some methods make it possible to determine illnesses of the soul and spirit. But it is not sufficient to determine an illness as in the case of an organic suffering which has been caused by improper nourishment, violent impact on the organism, etc.

It is much more difficult to study the causes of emotional and mental illnesses. It requires, as I have already pointed out several times, a vast knowledge of the psyche of people generally and of the individual in particular. It is not sufficient to establish that certain emotions and ways of expressing something are characterised by particular modes of behaviour.

The cause of the behaviour must be pin-pointed. This is a big step forward in the study of the psyche. Science has ground to a halt in mid-stream because it does not go further or believes that it cannot go further. Of course, there is a difference if one regards the matter from an earthly point of view or from here. No doctor on earth sees the causes as we do. Therefore, he cannot be held responsible for the fact that medical science is groping around in the dark.

This is why I will tell you how to penetrate the mystery of the psyche. Quite a lot has been written about it so I will just summarise it.

The influences of the emotional life, as earthly science calls it, are in accordance with past incarnations, the level of spiritual development, and the intensity of the individual's free will.

The soul has no life of its own as one would be led to believe by the words "emotional life." It is not an independent factor, but rather vital energy – or the seat of vital energy – and therefore the seat of the emotional life. But not emotional in the sense of pure sensitivity; rather the ability to react to every outer and inner influence.

The degree of reaction determines the greater or lesser receptivity in every respect, whether it is the functional activity of the organism or a connecting link to the mental plane and the activity of the mental powers. The more – or less – developed soul, capable of greater or lesser reaction, certainly develops further in the course of earthly life, but its foundation exists at birth. It is from this given basis that it must build up.

As I have said, not every spirit entity is sufficiently advanced to recognise the value of progress and focus its complete attention on striving for advanced development. This consideration must make it clear where the doctor's task must begin.

We have discussed the fact that the development of soul and spirit, despite their close ties, does not always keep pace, and that therefore great vital energy and the distinct ability to grasp the influences on the soul and the spirit could coincide with a far weaker spirit which is not in a position to utilise the emotional output of the soul.

Yes, I can well see that it is very difficult for the earthly doctor to make a correct diagnosis in this area and restore the necessary balance between soul and spirit. Earthly life with its material concepts, its rat race for possessions, for recognition and power in great as in little things, is so far removed from spiritual concepts, from the necessity to be aware of the infinite cosmos, that at present it may appear to be impossible to achieve tangible results in this field.

But what is principally necessary in order to do so is the total conviction of the doctor that between this world and the next there are no solid boundaries, that correlations and interaction are possible and absolutely necessary if one wishes to penetrate the mental and emotional realms and remedy the outlook on life of abnormal individuals. The first task is to explore the deeply concealed life plan, the blueprint that the person brought with him at birth. And, as I have said, to do so it is necessary to get to know his way of life and his concrete views on life, which are expressed not by what he says, but what he does. Of course, this depends on the doctor's ability of projection, because what must also be taken into consideration are the outside influences, the possible pressure of the surroundings and the economic conditions which pertain.

From this one can see that a hard and fast rule is barely possible, the more so because everybody is individual and cannot be compared with another person. In my earthly practice I never came across two people who were so similar that I could subject them to the same treatment. Everybody reacts differently to what he is told and how it is told, and the same conclusions can never be deduced from a reaction. Two people can react in exactly the same way to an unfriendly word or reprimand. Both may accept it in silence, but the one will have a feeling of enormous resistance, opposition and dislike, the other, one of resignation, understanding, even thankfulness. This goes to show that everybody must be considered individually, even if the basic methods of examination are the same or similar.

Now we will go one step further and presume that we already know in which direction the life line runs. An artist, for example, has pronounced inclinations to higher things that far exceed the daily round, even in early childhood. The people around him have no understanding for this because material results are far more highly valued and hinder the growing person in his planned development. This will soon be recognised if the teacher, or if necessary the doctor, observes him correctly.

A true artist does not strive alone on earth. Every help from the world beyond surrounds him and tries to break the bonds. If a person who is misguided in this way is brought to a capable doctor, one may be sure that help will be provided by good guides. The doctor or teacher to whom the child has been entrusted should recognise this important task. The doctor will make the right findings without realising that helping spirits are around him, trying hard to eliminate mistakes.

This brings me to the crux of the problem. I don't just want to explain what is wrong, but wish to point the way to be followed so that suffering mankind can find some relief.

Just as every single patient can call on his guides from the world beyond and put himself in their hands, so every good doctor can do his work for the benefit of mankind if he knows that help from the hereafter is at his disposal.

Have the courage to act, and do not be ashamed to ask invisible people questions. Try it and you will become masters in your profession and rise to the very highest calling! The prerequisite is, of course, singular professional ethics and the absolute will and resolution to want only what is good and seek to understand truth, without personal benefit and material gain. This follows automatically if selfless absorption in the calling is the basis of work.

The impact on soul and spirit from the world beyond is as diverse as the influences in earthly existence; it is only that these are visible and can be appraised, cultivated or opposed whereas the invisible ones have to be investigated and recognised in quite a different way to be mastered.

Why should one not seek invisible friends in order to combat invisible foes and link up with them to do good and banish evil from the world?

Through my medium, Grete, I shall still prove much of what I say if serious researchers ask me to.

This was the first indication. I shall say more about it in the next instalment.

Positive and negative possession and its treatment.

IN my last message I said it should be possible to call upon invisible friends to combat invisible foes.

Now it is necessary to examine precisely who could be considered invisible foes and when this has been established, to check which friends one may call upon to combat them and who has been allowed to do so. Many mistakes can be made in this connection if the procedure is not one hundred per cent correct, or people who are not called to do so attempt to establish contact.

Let us examine one question after the other and answer it. First, who are invisible enemies? Not every illness can be traced back to alien influences – at least not directly – and so for this study we can eliminate all those bodily sufferings which are brought on by an incorrect life-style, physical inheritance or mechanical impact. In other words, all visible causes.

We are concerned only with those psychic diseases that cannot be traced to influences. By this I mean after all influences from the environment, life situations and personal behaviour connected with will and intent have been discounted. To be more precise, only those illnesses which oppress the soul and which the patient, with the best will in the world, is powerless to resist; illnesses which are incompatible with the nature of the person according to his normal conduct and cannot be explained.

For example, depressions which occur without visible reason. This does not mean to say that every depression in the generally accepted sense must have a definite reason. A lack of positive influences and wasted effort, even without serious set-backs, can lead to depression which is caused by a person's thoughts and feelings because his situation and achievements are way below his aims. To this can be added wrong thoughts brought about by incorrect examples or the effort to overcome an inferiority complex; both these are invisible battles that only occur in the patient's imagination. All these illnesses that fall into the above listed behaviour patterns can be eliminated.

In these cases, it is in the main sufficient to awaken the will and the energy to live, to generate self-confidence and draw forth all the healing powers from the patient himself. We will discuss these methods of treatment case by case and examine many of them until everything is quite clear and a good working platform has been established for successful treatment.

This leaves us with psychic illnesses which do not originate within the patient, but have been injected into him. Illnesses in the true sense of the word they are not, rather burdens imposed by other sick souls. Once they have been removed, the results are full recoveries. As we can see, it is actually easier to heal such psychic illnesses than it is to help those people who have to battle against their own abnormal attitudes and mistakes. But do not let us make the mistake of minimising matters; it is easy to establish the cure if the diagnosis has been correct. The difficulty for the doctor on earth lies in the fact that he cannot – as we do – see the foreign spirit entity which has possessed an earthly person to indulge his own obsession.

But let us consider things from a positive aspect. How many artists are there in the realm of music and painting and, if we will, also technology, who with their human energies would hardly be able to achieve their outstanding results if helping spirits did not use them to realise their own creative desires?

I possess my medium Grete in this manner, but take great care to test in how far I may use her energies for my work without overburdening and making too high demands on her.

Just as good, sensible spirit entities called to impart information to mankind make use of auxiliaries, so too underdeveloped spirit entities have the desire to make their mark in the material world and search for ways and means to assert themselves.

Quite frequently individuals are harassed by several such spirits, naturally without knowing it. But they are people who are unstable and not in tune with their own lifestyle. They yearn for diversions and exaggerated tranquillising or stimulating sensations. Dependent entirely on the level of development of the individual, such entities find each other. The one party has not yet attained its spiritual maturity and therefore the necessary resistance, and the other, the insight and realisation. These entities are the most dangerous for weak, earthly people.

It is a different matter with people who are very mediumistically predisposed and have reached a mature stage of development. Spirit entities seek their help which they believe they need because they simply are unable to cope with the situation in which they find themselves. After their departure from the material world they wander around, do not find their way into the world beyond and are unhappy because they cannot make themselves noticed in the earthly sphere.

I know from personal experience how painful this is. Admittedly, I needed only a short transition period. I was received in the radiance of the other-worldly sphere. Although I did not want to believe it at first, I could find the way with my own energy. I say with my own energy, but it was with the help of good spirit entities whom I was prepared to believe and not oppose.

Spirit entities who cannot find the way on their own and are not prepared to believe their good guides, hang on to earthly people with all their might, appealing to them to explain things to them and help them. Such lamentations are a great strain for people, in the same way as the complaints and misery of earthly people who are very close to each other.

But for earthly partners there are words and deeds to overcome the misery; it is a tangible pain. The misery of a departed spirit is a different matter. People with mediumistic powers should learn to guide such erring spirit entities of those departed onto the right path. With kind words and affectionate encouragement they must try to make it clear that they now live in a different realm and can achieve nothing by continuing to cling to them. Obsessive souls must be handled differently. They have to be dealt with energetically to be kept at bay for after they have been expelled from an alien body they often return.

I have mentioned several times that there are means of expelling possessing spirits and that apart from a strengthening of will – the will of the one possessed – mechanical influences like electricity can give results.

Primarily what is necessary is the recognition of possession by an alien being and the consequences, of such, which cannot be ascribed to the earthly person involved. It will soon be possible to do this. The prerequisite is that my words are believed. If a patient is quite willing to renounce a craving and, uninfluenced by earthly means, is not afraid of any danger and spares no pain to give himself completely to misdemeanours and exaggerations which are in complete contradiction to his normal nature, then it is surely in order to apply methods which are not in the text books of neurology and psychiatry but belong there, alongside the essays on nerve reflexes and neuroses.

One contradiction needs to be explained. I spoke about unstable people and the fact that underdeveloped spirit entities only attach themselves to corresponding humans. But on the other hand I mentioned about the contrast in the nature of an obsessed person whose cravings are quite incompatible with his overall character. As has already been stated, it is necessary to differentiate between the social level, the standing in the material sense, and the spiritual development which an earthly person is only seldom in a position to appreciate.

The picture a doctor on earth receives of a person is one formed and influenced by environment, custom, education and intellectual formation. The best character study is often in flagrant contradiction to the emotional and spiritual level of development. Harmony between soul and spirit entity is lacking. Therefore disturbing, destructive influences are allowed free entry.

How much there is for a doctor to learn about the nature of an individual if he wants to do good and help him to progress. He will soon see that his possibilities of succeeding are extremely limited if he relies only on his own knowledge and ideas. Enough for today.

The influence of the world beyond on the material world and the development of mankind.

YESTERDAY we noted that there are various abnormal psychic attitudes, illnesses and stresses which can hamper and disturb people in heir earthly careers. At a later stage I will discuss the study generally and specify the most common occurrences.

I will begin with the stresses caused by foreign spirit entities who seize control of a person's body without his knowledge and either crowd out the rightful spirit entity or force it to give certain manifestations of life; these are in complete contradiction to the wishes and intentions of the individual concerned and have to be carried out through no fault of his.

I will be asked how this is actually to be understood. It is very simple.

We have learned that man's will is free, but it is open to influence and guidance. This finds expression in every degree up to outside compulsion; it is to be seen in legal and judicial education, but always according to cause and necessity.

When a person is possessed, he also cannot exert his free will, but in this case we are unable to identify the cause, the motivation, the obstruction or the stimulus.

Nobody can disengage his free will voluntarily. He can leave off doing something that he originally wanted to do, but conversely without exerting his will he cannot bring about an activity or do things that are foreign to his nature.

More often than one can believe, people are guided and misguided by foreign powers. They can barely believe that what they are doing has not been ordered by their brain and is not of their own accord.

It is a difficult matter which, as I have already indicated, affects jurisdiction and has an important influence on the judgement of atrocity and compulsion. Nevertheless, this difficult problem must be tackled energetically. It should be made clear where the limits are and how they can be established. Only psychologists can venture to discuss this with the judiciary and medical experts, and smooth the way with the help of guides from the other world.

A person possessed by an alien spirit entity in a devastating, inconsiderate manner, shows reactions which are strange or exceed the normal measure of healthy people. Generally a healthy person – I would say every person – knows the limits of a normal way of living and naturally endeavours to maintain these and ensure his progress. This endeavour is quite unconscious; it is inborn and lies hidden deep within.

The environment that he grows into often brings other limits into play. Nevertheless, the transgression of normal limits is not necessarily to be inferred from this. In fact, very often an exaggeration in any given direction creates an inner resistance which, sooner or later, seeks to attain its goal and wants free development within whatever framework the individual has chosen according to the programme he has brought with him.

We must always bear in mind that we are not discussing totally underdeveloped, backward spirit entities; we are dealing with those who come into the material world with the best of intentions and the wish to progress. Not all of them, however, have the strength to resist evil and obstructive influences. It is the material philosophy of life which primarily hampers their progress and deflects them from their path.

It is not right to pity these souls and assume that it is a monumental crime if they do not fulfil what they had undertaken to do. Admittedly the realisation is bitter when, from here, they see how little progress they have made.

We want to discuss those weak souls who need our help and for whom it is worthwhile to take trouble and make every effort so that they attain what they set out to do. I know from experience how many people suffer on this account and how many doctors try to help them.

In my own practice, I often realised that what a person said or did was not a reflection of his character or ways. But I was forced to accept it as his reaction to life and therefore had to take him very firmly to task on that account and reprimand him. Today it is obvious how very wrong I was. This is why I want to try and teach my successors; to help them and point out that others are responsible and not those who have been delivered up to law or those in treatment.

In obvious cases it will be possible to find a solution without the help of otherworldly guides. It only needs the courage to face the issue squarely and tackle it with the appropriate means. Medicines, cures and psychic treatment will not bring relief. Only exorcism will. Before the doctor dares to take this step everything offered in the way of treatment for abnormal behaviour must be tried in case this emanates from the patient himself. But always with kindness and sympathetic understanding, guided by the thought that harsh words are the wrong approach if alien influences are the cause. If all forms of psychic treatment are to no avail or there has been a relapse without a reason, there only remains the world beyond and its helping spirits.

No doctor need fear to be drawn into the spell of such disturbers of the peace if he begins to do battle with them. Active dabbling in Spiritualism is what endangers people; this means invocation and contact with spirits in an unauthorised manner because of a craving for sensation or superficial interest, but not honest dialogue with spirit entities who have failed to appreciate their situation and make themselves and others unhappy.

Every positive activity aiming only to do good must have a beneficial result. The exorcised spirit as well as the person who was possessed will both find happiness.

Above all, it is necessary that at long last the understanding dawns and takes root that the earthly world is so closely linked to the world beyond that the one flows into the other and cannot be regarded as separate because both depend on each other.

Progress in the earthly sphere cannot be considered without the influence and help of the world beyond. Conversely, the earthly world is the touchstone for the development of spirit entities who have sought progress in the fourth dimension and now want to prove it. To do this, they have to serve, strive and suffer again on earth. This is such an obvious truth that it barely needs to be emphasised.

But the immaturity of the earthly world in astonishing dimensions becomes glaringly obvious when it seeks to ignore all natural laws and disregards what comes to it from realms that are still unknown. I have not been called to instruct natural science and introduce new teachings in this field, although today I would be able to refute many things that I learned in school about the world and the universe and replace them with the correct interpretation. It would certainly not be difficult from this advanced viewpoint, as I can see further and realise where we err and must make corrections.

Many mistakes can be forgiven and need no atonement. They are honest interpretations caused by a limited horizon and are surely not easy to renounce. But the moment interpretations reach the stage that people see themselves as divine beings of the first order then the stage of inexcusable arrogance has been reached and leads to an aversion to truth. By this, I mean resistance to what is true and which the little earthly beings should accept with alacrity and goodwill. As soon as people are honestly convinced that they are very small, insignificant beings in the infinite universe, the beautiful dream is no more. Their efforts must be directed towards goals other than those of power, possession and personal recognition.

The knowledge that it is not man, the material citizen of the world, who guides the destiny of the earthly realm must be accepted. The knowledge that in order to make spiritual progress, contact with Omnipotence, who guides the destiny of the world, is both possible and necessary must reshape peoples' way of thinking more and more and lead to a new and quite different lifestyle. This is the prerequisite that will bring order to any intellectual activity.

People will attain the ability to enlighten departed spirits in such a way that it will put an end to their devastating ability to terrorise humanity, both internally and externally. All indications point in this direction and soon – although perhaps not according to earthly chronology – a change may be expected to take place. So much for today.

Dr. Nowotny offers his help.
The correct measure of lifetasks.

TODAY, we will discuss how to establish and put into effect what I described in the previous chapter. I will point the way without discussing it in detail. A serious researcher will bring us a case and with my help undertake a correct exorcism. Afterwards he shall be able to establish that the patient is cured.

But I must point out again that it is not impossible that a person cured in this way will again be bothered by spirit entities unless, after the cure, he remains for a considerable period of time under the supervision of his doctor and his own energy, his soul, is so strengthened that he feels sufficient power of resistance within himself and can muster it against unwanted intruders.

With such a demonstration the first great step would have been taken. But not the first since the beginning of this world. Oh no, far more advanced civilisations of earlier times have come to the same conclusion and made contact with the spirits for the well-being of mankind.

There is good literature on the subject by doctors of a distant continent who have undertaken psychic and spiritual healing with the help of good mediums. Their work, although on a small scale, was very beneficial and should serve as educational material and a guide for psychiatrists in preference to traditional text books.

What I am trying to say is that I really am not introducing anything new through my findings and doctrines. I only wish to extend help and would like to be a guide from the world beyond, just as these great men served as guides in their earthly life.

As I have said, it is easy for me to make a diagnosis in a case like this because I can see the incriminating spirit entities. I therefore cannot make a mistake, and the results must be correct.

I will revert to this theme again, but now I want to introduce a new subject which has found too little attention: emotional suffering which can be traced to ignorance of the real reason for life and which constitutes the major section of all emotional illnesses.

We have already indicated how important it is to have a positive, healthy outlook on life and to think out a point of view for the duties it entails. They are there for everybody, whether he be important or insignificant, and they are equally difficult. Their mastery requires every ounce of strength, regardless of class or material level. How many people suffer because they have to live in bad material circumstances without recognising that their duties are adjusted and apportioned in a way suited to these very circumstances and have to be carried out to the best of their available abilities.

It is all a matter of mental outlook; it is the doctor's duty to impart this information. Let me present a lesson to make myself clear. People are of the opinion that they have to make every effort to improve their happiness in this world and heighten their well-being. With this viewpoint they see the justification for their behaviour, for their striving for honour, fame, prestige, possessions and money.

When a patient sees that he has no opportunity of acquiring these desirable – desirable in his estimation – attributes, although his spiritual maturity, education and schooling would indicate that he was qualified for this so-called advanced standard of life, he comes into conflict with himself and loses the correct attitude to his life-line. There has to be intervention.

It must become common knowledge that man is not on earth only to do justice to his social background, but rather, apart from the necessary adaption to his surroundings, he is there to fulfil his tasks which, according to his blueprint are, I might say, placed in his lap.

If a person is convinced that nothing is coincidence, that the law of cause and effect and self-imposed destiny mark the life-line, then he will tackle the most difficult problems with equanimity and tranquillity and know how to master with confidence that which inner resistance and doubts about prevailing justness would never let him accomplish.

Nobody is given more difficult tasks to master than he is able to accomplish. The absolute conviction of this fundamental truth may be an indication to many a person that great tasks – of course I don't mean those which are purely born of matter and only lead to material success – dominate the picture of life. I refer to such tasks which stand for spiritual progress and are performed for the benefit of all mankind, or even for one person.

The task in hand permits everybody to assess his own level of development. It will give him happiness and joy that he is able to do so and has been called upon to perform such great and difficult work. Good guides and helpers of mankind should impart such knowledge to their protégés who despair at their reason for living and their goals in life.

Self-confidence does not grow with the mastering of tasks that are below the level of accomplishment of the individual, but only with efforts that necessitate a person's total commitment and personality. This is another basic truth of life which is worthy of notice.

It is not of great significance whether or not a person feels up to the demands of life. He must only have the courage to tackle things and try to achieve more than he believes his abilities are capable of. I have strayed somewhat from the theme. But it is of great importance in connection with a correct concept of life to apply one's energies where they are needed, and where there are weaknesses that need to be overcome.

As I have already said, every person has a concept of life which is sufficient unto himself. This is why the basic truth must be adapted to this way of thinking and the dictate for achievement and striving must be carefully weighed. Demands set too high will cause discouragement; if they are not high enough, there will be uncertainty with regard to the set task which is not commensurate with the available energy.

But the basis for a successful treatment must be the correct knowledge of the life-line and the conviction of the value of a sad, oppressive life.

There is hardly a patient with a higher level of development who will argue with this point of view. We know from experience that depressions, I mean those originating within the individual, occur more often in people who are spiritually more highly developed than in primitive and underdeveloped people. The latter don't waste much time thinking about their goals in earthly life. Those who are spiritually more mature feel the urge to progress within, but cannot find the path.

Up to now, as I have already said, material success in life was the measure for a person's value, for the judgement as to what extent life's goal had been attained. Competency is a concept that only exists in connection with matter, although one should deal very cautiously with this attribute. Yes, one may speak of competent people if, in addition to their spiritual and emotional development, they also know how to achieve material success.

But radically different concepts must gain ground if a proper judgement of qualities is to be achieved and suffering people helped out of their impasse.

In my earthly practice I often established that people who lived in the greatest prosperity and had every material benefit they could desire were in a deplorable emotional state. One considered them ungrateful as they were so richly endowed and had no financial problems. It seemed a far-fetched request to Fate to want still more.

But this is a wrong interpretation for all the material goods of this world cannot replace what these people lack to fulfil the life tasks that they have set themselves. Once again I point out that a person must learn to recognise that all tasks are in keeping with his abilities. With this conviction he is able to master them. Discontent with material possessions is caused by the fact that a person cannot use his powers which enable him to master higher tasks.

Therefore, on the one hand, the doctor has to stimulate trust and self-confidence; on the other, energy and creative happiness, solidarity with the community and renunciation of material wishes. But in every instance the individual has to be thoroughly studied and his degree of spiritual and emotional maturity as well as his attitude to the community must be clearly defined so that the right measure is found for his guidance and the appraisal of his energies and achievements.

We will close today. Tomorrow we will again begin to study the causes of emotional suffering in greater detail.